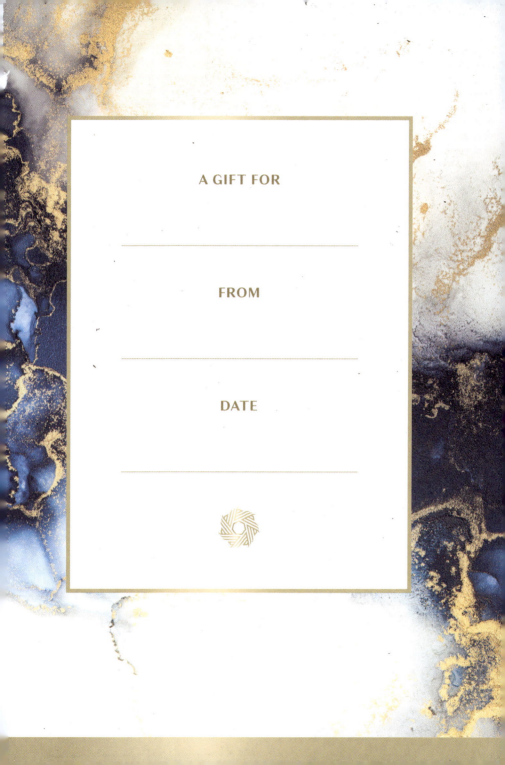

A GIFT FOR

_____

FROM

_____

DATE

_____

DR. DAVID JEREMIAH

*NEW YORK TIMES* BESTSELLING AUTHOR

# WHAT
# GOD
# PROMISES
# YOU

## SEVEN TRUTHS

That Will Change the Way You Live

THOMAS NELSON

*Since 1798*

Published by Thomas Nelson, 501 Nelson Place, Nashville, TN 37214, USA.
Thomas Nelson is a registered trademark of HarperCollins Christian Publishing, Inc.

Published in association with Yates & Yates, www.yates2.com.

Thomas Nelson titles may be purchased in bulk for educational, business, fundraising, or sales promotional use. For information, please email SpecialMarkets@ThomasNelson.com.

Unless otherwise noted, Scripture quotations are taken from the New King James Version®. Copyright © 1982 by Thomas Nelson. Used by permission. All rights reserved.

Scripture quotations marked NIV are taken from the Holy Bible, New International Version®, NIV®. Copyright © 1973, 1978, 1984, 2011 by Biblica, Inc.® Used by permission of Zondervan. All rights reserved worldwide. www.zondervan.com. The "NIV" and "New International Version" are trademarks registered in the United States Patent and Trademark Office by Biblica, Inc.®

HarperCollins Publishers, Macken House, 39/40 Mayor Street Upper, Dublin 1, D01 C9W8, Ireland (https://www.harpercollins.com)

Images used under license from Shutterstock.com and stock.adobe.com.

Cover design: Sabryna Lugge
Interior design: Sabryna Lugge and Kristen Sasamoto

ISBN 978-1-4002-3049-5 (HC)
ISBN 978-1-4002-3051-8 (audiobook)
ISBN 978-1-4002-3050-1 (eBook)

*Printed in India*

25 26 27 28 29 MAN 10 9 8 7 6 5 4 3 2 1

# CONTENTS

*You will keep him in perfect peace,*
*Whose mind is stayed on You,*
*Because he trusts in You.*

Isaiah 26:3

# THE PROMISE KEEPER

*The LORD always keeps his promises;*
*he is gracious in all he does.*
Psalm 145:13 NLT

SEVERAL POWERFUL MOVEMENTS AND ORGANIZA-tions have energized the church over the course of my lifetime. One of the most exciting was the Promise Keepers era. The movement started in 1990 under the leadership of Bill McCartney. At the time, Bill was the head football coach at the University of Colorado, which had just lost the NCAA championship game. One day as Bill was driving to a Fellowship of Christian Athletes banquet with his friend Dave Wardell, the pair lamented the spiritual state of men in America and how it was impacting our nation's families.

Importantly, Bill and Dave didn't just lament the

problem. They decided to do something about it. Within a year, Promise Keepers had gathered four thousand men at the University of Colorado's basketball arena to worship God and pray for a movement that would galvanize American men. In the following years, tens of thousands of men met in stadiums all across the country. And then, in 1997, more than five hundred thousand men gathered in Washington, DC, to "stand in the gap" on behalf of their wives, their families, and their communities.

The Promise Keepers movement is still going strong today, and one of the core tenets of the organization is what they call the "7 promises of a Promise Keeper." I won't list all seven, but they include promises such as "A Promise Keeper is committed to honoring Jesus Christ through worship, prayer, and obedience to God's Word in the power of the Holy Spirit," and "A Promise Keeper understands that Jesus calls him to be His hands and feet, serving others with integrity. He purposely lifts up the leadership of the church and his nation in prayer."[1]

It's wonderful for followers of Jesus, both men and women, to make promises to God and then keep them. Thankfully, that's not the only direction it works. Our God is a promise keeper—one who never fails to uphold His Word.

Similarly, our God is a promise maker. He has packed Scripture full of promises made by Him and deliverable to us. Many of those promises pertain to two realities: the failings of this world and our future in heaven. But as we'll see in the pages that follow, God's promises cover a broad range of topics and have a powerful influence on our lives.

We're going to explore seven of these promises over the next seven chapters. Choosing which promises to examine has been no easy task! After all, thousands of God's promises to us are stuffed within the pages of His Word. Which ones should we focus on first?

Thankfully, King David has done us a favor by writing Psalm 37, a song packed with reflections on God's promises. We'll use that psalm as the specific jumping-off point for our general survey of God's promises. Doing so will allow us to jump into these seven promises:

- the promise of provision
- the promise of forgiveness
- the promise of peace
- the promise of protection
- the promise of purpose
- the promise of relationship
- the promise of eternity

What a list! Take a look at these promises and then ask yourself: What else do I need? What could I possibly desire that is not included in these seven promises?

One more thought before we get started: I'd like to give you a challenge as you engage these pages. It would be easy to work your way through this resource as a "promise reader"—as someone who becomes more aware of God's promises on the level of information. That's not good enough. That's not helpful enough.

So don't be a promise reader. Instead, be a promise claimer!

What do I mean? Well, as we've seen, God makes promises in His Word, but we have to claim them. A promise not claimed and acted upon has the same practical effect as a promise never made. If I promise to help you whenever you call me, but you never call, you never receive the benefit of my promise.

In my life, then, God is the promise maker, and I am the promise claimer. The same is true for you.

There is no single list of God's promises in Scripture. Instead, we find them as we read from Genesis to Revelation. Whether spoken explicitly or revealed implicitly, all of God's promises are rooted in His character.

For instance, "I will never leave you nor forsake you" (Hebrews 13:5) is an explicit promise to all Christians. But God's promise directly to the apostle Paul—"My grace is sufficient for you, for My strength is made perfect in weakness" (2 Corinthians 12:9)—is also an implicit promise to all believers. Paul spoke for all of us when he said, "For when I am weak, then I am strong [in Christ]" (v. 10). If the power of Christ was available to Paul, it is likewise available to us by implication.

In my life, then,
God is the promise
maker, and I am the
promise claimer. The
same is true for you.

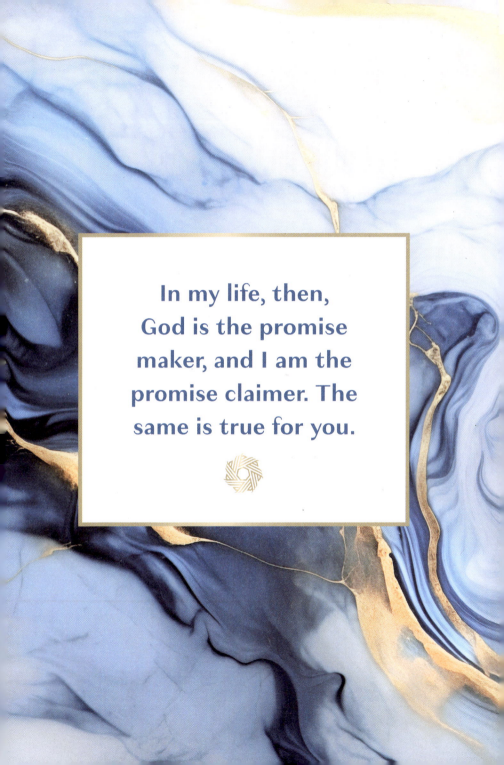

Therefore, our task as we work through these pages is to know the character of God so well that we can take His very being and presence as a promise—one made incarnate in the person of Jesus Christ.

Are you ready?

CHAPTER ONE

# GOD PROMISES YOU
# PROVISION

*Delight yourself also in the L*ORD*,*
*And He shall give you the desires of your heart.*
Psalm 37:4

AS FOUNDER OF A SOCIAL MEDIA MONITORING COM-pany, Marcel LeBrun had a lot of experience talking (and posting) about the homelessness crisis plaguing his city of Fredericton in New Brunswick, Canada. Everyone wanted to argue about the issue, but of course arguments produce very few results.

"We wanted to make a dent in the challenge that we have here in Fredericton," said LeBrun, which meant doing more than talking. He realized, "If we want to actually make a meaningful difference, we have to build some houses."[1]

LeBrun had the chance to do just that when he sold

his business, and he jumped at the opportunity. After purchasing a sixty-acre piece of property on the outskirts of Fredericton, LeBrun set up a warehouse and began building tiny homes. Lots of tiny homes. Altogether, the 12 Neighbours community offers ninety-nine homes for those in the Fredericton community experiencing homelessness.

Each home has a full-service kitchen, living room, bedroom, bathroom, porch, and solar power. And each home represents a second chance for an individual or family in need of help.

The 12 Neighbours community also provides more than housing. LeBrun has set up businesses within the community that offer employment to residents, including a coffee shop and a silk-screen printing shop. The goal is to provide opportunities not only for work but for residents of the community to interact and engage with the broader society of Fredericton.

"I see myself as a community builder," says LeBrun. "Really what we're doing here is not just building a little community, but we're building a community in a city, like how do we help our city be better?"[2]

Couldn't we all use a little help these days? You may not be experiencing homelessness—and I certainly pray that is never the case for you or your family members. Even so, many are struggling with financial burdens.

Younger people are often weighed down by student loans and sluggish wages. Older generations have become increasingly encumbered by the rising cost of health care and the expenses of aging parents. All of us have been hit by inflation and skyrocketing prices. If you had told me ten years ago that a carton of eggs would cost seven or eight dollars, I never would have believed it!

The Bible is right when it declares, "Cast but a glance at riches, and they are gone, for they will surely sprout wings and fly off to the sky like an eagle" (Proverbs 23:5 NIV). We've always known money has wings, but only in recent years have we begun to truly comprehend its wingspan. The COVID-19 pandemic was an economic wake-up call in addition to a medical crisis. Natural disasters such as fires, floods, earthquakes, and hurricanes have ravaged entire regions of our nation and of the world—at great expense. Wars continue to drain our coffers. And now more than ever, huge troves of resources have become concentrated in the hands of a few individuals and organizations.

The stock market keeps going up, but many more realistic indicators of our quality of life continue trending down. As a result, it's easy to feel down and out—downcast, downtrodden, and down on our luck.

In such a season as this, it's critical that we focus on God's promise of provision. And as providence would have it, that's the first promise mentioned by David in Psalm 37. Take a look:

> Trust in the LORD, and do good;
> Dwell in the land, and feed on His
> faithfulness.
> Delight yourself also in the LORD,
> And He shall give you the desires of your
> heart. (vv. 3–4)

Later in the same psalm, David added a few additional thoughts to God's promise of provision in the lives of His people:

> I have been young, and now am old;
> Yet I have not seen the righteous forsaken,
> Nor his descendants begging bread.
> He is ever merciful, and.lends;
> And his descendants are blessed.
> (vv. 25–26)

Don't overlook these wonderful assurances! Because you are God's child, He has promised to be faithful to you and meet your needs. Scripture promises that you can "feed on His faithfulness" and that "He shall give you the desires of your heart." Scripture promises that

Because you are
God's child, He has
promised to be
faithful to you and
meet your needs.

you will not be forsaken or left empty. Instead, you and your descendants will be "blessed."

Let's take a deeper look at the reality of God's provision in our lives. I'd like to do so by working together to recognize the different ways God has promised to provide for us in Scripture and then by exploring what it means for us to receive that provision each day.

## Recognizing God's Promise of Provision

Looking through history, we would be hard-pressed to find a group of people more dependent on God's provision than the Israelites, who escaped from Egypt and traversed the wilderness for forty years on their way to the promised land. As you may remember, this was not a small collection of people. Scripture says six hundred thousand men escaped through the Red Sea, besides women and children (Exodus 12:37), which means the *nation* of Israel was on the march during and after the exodus—a nation of between one and two million people.

That's a lot of mouths to feed! Not to mention the Israelites were moving through territory that was both unfamiliar and unforgiving. They were accosted by difficult weather, dangerous animals, and enemy armies. They were far from home and often far from hope.

Despite all these obstacles and more, God provided.

He gave the Israelites manna and quail for food. He gave them water from a rock and led them to life-saving wells. He gave them His own presence and power to guide them in the form of a pillar of cloud by day and a pillar of fire by night. In short, God took care of His chosen people—His children. And He continues to do so even to this very day.

> **God took care of His chosen people—His children. And He continues to do so even to this very day.**

The Bible is filled with similar stories of God's provision. Page after page, verse after verse reveals the lengths our heavenly Father will go to meet the needs of His children—and the joy He receives in doing so for His own sake. Consider these examples:

- When Abraham needed a sacrifice on Mount Moriah, God provided a ram caught in a thicket (Genesis 22:6–19).
- When Elijah hid from Ahab and Jezebel near the Brook Cherith, a squadron of ravens brought him bread and meat day and night (1 Kings 17:1–6).
- When Joseph and Mary needed emergency funds to flee to Egypt, the magi arrived with gold, frankincense, and myrrh (Matthew 2:7–15).
- When Peter needed to pay his taxes, Jesus sent a coin in the correct amount through the mouth of a fish (Matthew 17:24–27).

One question you may have is: What *type* of provision does God offer? In other words, what specifically can He and does He provide in our lives? What types of needs does He meet?

First, God meets our material needs. This includes food, clothing, shelter, and more. Jesus made that clear in His Sermon on the Mount:

"Therefore do not worry, saying, 'What shall we eat?' or 'What shall we drink?' or 'What shall we wear?' For after all these things the Gentiles seek.

For your heavenly Father knows that you need all these things. But seek first the kingdom of God and His righteousness, and all these things shall be added to you." (Matthew 6:31–33)

Those of us living in America may not think about such needs as often as those living in other parts of the globe (or at other times in history). We may take it for granted that our material needs are covered each day. We may even neglect to be grateful for the roof over our heads and the food in our pantry and the clothes in our closets.

One of the dangers of living in such a prosperous time and such a wealthy nation is that our perception of reality can become warped in ways that twist our understanding. For example, we may begin to think that money is the source of provision for our material needs— that money is responsible for our food, clothing, shelter, and more. When we start thinking that way, it's easy to believe we can only be secure by gaining more money. Or that we are dependent on money for our peace and fulfillment. For happiness.

Sadly, many in our culture have bought into that lie. A recent study revealed that 60 percent of Americans believe money can buy happiness. That number rose to 72 percent of millennials and 67 percent of those in Gen Z. More than that, the respondents were willing to put a price tag on happiness: $1.2 million, which means the

God cares not only
for our minds and our
thoughts, but also our
hearts. He provides peace
when we feel anxious.
He provides hope when
we feel downtrodden.
He provides comfort
when we are grieving.
He provides love and
connection when we
feel lost and alone.

average person in America is under the impression that if they could scrape together $1.2 million in their bank account or brokerage firm or even stuffed under their mattress, they would finally be happy.[3]

The problem, as we've already seen, is that money has wings. It flies away. It doesn't last. That means if we pin our happiness and security on our financial performance, they won't last. They'll be gone before we know it.

God, on the other hand, does last. He will never leave us nor forsake us, which means He is our ideal source of provision for every need.

Second, and speaking of happiness, God meets our emotional needs. Notice what the apostle Paul wrote to the church in Philippi:

> Be anxious for nothing, but in everything by prayer and supplication, with thanksgiving, let your requests be made known to God; and the peace of God, which surpasses all understanding, *will guard your hearts and minds through Christ Jesus.* (Philippians 4:6–7, emphasis added)

God cares not only for our minds and our thoughts, but also our hearts. He provides peace when we feel anxious. He provides hope when we feel downtrodden. He provides comfort when we are grieving. He provides love and connection when we feel lost and alone.

David said it this way: "The LORD is close to the brokenhearted and saves those who are crushed in spirit" (Psalm 34:18 NIV).

Finally, God meets our spiritual needs. These words from 2 Peter have been especially meaningful in my life and ministry in recent years: "His divine power has given us everything we need for a godly life through our knowledge of him who called us by his own glory and goodness. Through these he has given us his very great and precious promises, so that through them you may participate in the divine nature, having escaped the corruption in the world caused by evil desires" (1:3–4 NIV).

God has given us everything we need not just for life but for godliness. For a righteous life. He has given us salvation—the forgiveness of sin purchased by the very blood of Jesus Christ. He has given us redemption and restoration. And He has given us the promise of eternity, which we'll discuss more deeply in chapter 7.

The bottom line is this: God has promised to provide everything we need. And He always keeps His promises.

## Receiving God's Promise of Provision

Let me remind you once more: God promises you provision. He has promised in many ways and in many passages of Scripture to provide for all of your needs—material, emotional, spiritual, and more. He alone is your certain source for provision, which means He is where you should always turn first when confronted with a need.

That leads to an important question: *What's our role in the process?* God is the provider, and we are the ones for whom He provides. Does that mean we become passive? Should we simply sit back and wait for God to give us what we need without any effort on our own part?

No. God provides, but we have a role in receiving His love and care and gifts and blessings. We have a part to play in His provision.

First and foremost, remember that God has promised to provide for His children. He has promised provision for those who are citizens of His kingdom in heaven even as we live and work and minister as residents of this world. Therefore, the first step we need to take in order to receive God's provision is to accept the free gift of salvation offered through the death and resurrection of Jesus Christ.

Beyond that decision, I'd like to offer five more steps you and I can take to actively receive what God has promised to provide.

1. *Communicate your needs.* Tell God about your needs, humbly and honestly. Talk with Him as your heavenly Father. Make it a matter of earnest

prayer to share your needs and requests and desires in the name of Jesus.

2. *Memorize key Scripture passages.* Commit God's promises to your heart so that they transform you and build your faith. Take a moment to review the Scripture passages listed in the previous section of this chapter. Which of those promises encouraged you most? Which ones inspired you? Write down those passages and commit them to memory. Claim those promises as part of yourself.

3. *Examine your past.* God is your provider now, and God has always been your provider in the past. So take a moment to make a list of the ways God has already provided for your needs. Write down examples—as many as you can—of moments and seasons when God stepped into your life as provider.

4. *Take a step.* As I mentioned earlier, God's provision should not render us passive. Therefore, if you are in a season of need right now, identify something you can do to move toward God's provision. Refuse to sit down and stew in worry. Doubt and anxiety are the tools of Satan. Instead, stand up and identify something you can do right now to present your needs to God or to move in the direction He is leading you. Think of the next logical step and take it, even if that step is a small one.

5. *Be generous.* As we give our shovelfuls to the Lord, He sends his truckloads to us. So when you experience a need, be conscious of your own opportunities to help provide for the needs of others.

Now, there's a chance you may be reading this chapter and thinking, *Dr. Jeremiah, I want to believe God's promise to provide for my needs, but I'm not seeing it. I have needs that are not being met, so what does that mean?*

That's an important question. It's a helpful question, and I'd like to answer it with a cooking metaphor. I'm not much of a chef myself, but I've been around enough masters of the kitchen to know that almost every good meal requires some heat to prepare. The stove. The oven. The boiling pot. These are necessary tools for any respectable cook.

Heat is a necessary tool for God as well. Not thermal heat, of course, but the heat of life. The heat of discomfort, sorrow, and pain. These are some of the ways He transforms the raw ingredients of who we are into the finished work of women and men who think and act like Christ.

Let me say this directly: Allowing us to experience temporary want (or unmet needs) is one of the ways God turns up the heat in our lives. It's one of the tools He uses to prepare us for what's to come. If you find yourself in such a season, the answer is not to get away from the heat. Instead, the answer is to trust the Chef. Trust the Master. Specifically, trust that His promises will be brought to bear in your life.

Harry Ironside experienced the heat of being in need on many occasions during his childhood years. He was one of the most popular preachers and prolific authors of the first half of the twentieth century—a man of great faith. Yet much of his godly zeal was kindled by watching his widowed mother, Sophia, trust God for daily provisions for her family.

Harry's father, John, an ardent soul-winner, passed away at age twenty-seven, leaving Sophia with two small boys and no income. On one occasion, she was expecting company for supper. Though her cupboard was nearly bare, she scraped together a meal with the little that remained. After the visitors left, she found under one of their plates a ten-dollar bill—a vast sum in those days. With eyes full of tears, she offered thanks to God.

Sometime later, the cupboard was again empty. Sophia gathered her two sons to the table for breakfast, but their plates were empty, and there was only water to drink. "We will give thanks, boys," she said. Closing her eyes, she claimed the promise of Isaiah 33:16: "Father, Thou hast promised in Thy Word, 'Your bread shall be given you, and your water shall be sure.' We have the water, and we thank Thee for it. And now, we trust Thee for the bread, or for that which will take its place."

Trust the Master.
Specifically, trust
that His promises
will be brought to
bear in your life.

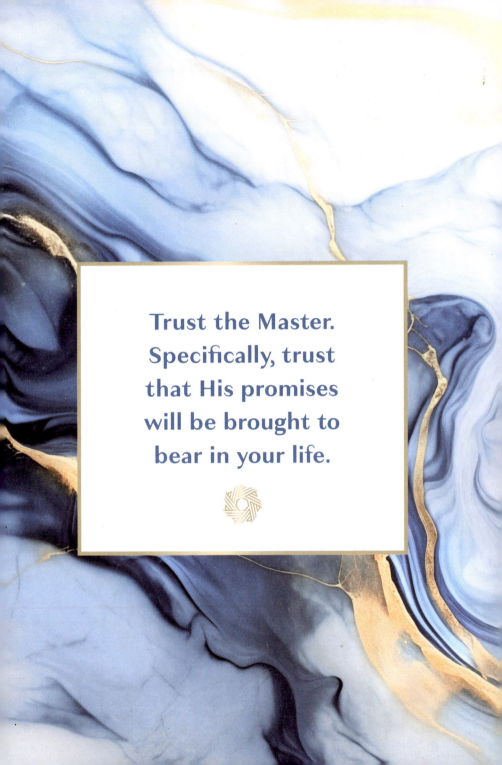

Just as she finished praying, the doorbell rang, and the boys ran to the door to find a man there. "Mrs. Ironside," he said, "I feel very bad. We have owed you for months for that dress you made for my wife. We've had no money to pay you. But just now we're harvesting our potatoes, and we wondered if you would take a bushel or two on account of the old bill."

"Indeed, I'll be glad to," replied Sophia.

In a few minutes, the potatoes were sizzling in the frying pan, and the boys had answered prayers for breakfast.[4]

None of us knows exactly what method God will choose to meet our needs. He is God, after all! He possesses infinite resources, and He is infinitely creative. There's no limit to the steps He may take to operate as our provider.

All of us can rest assured that God will keep His promise to provide.

*Heavenly Father, I trust You to provide for my needs. I commit to letting go of my own efforts to provide for myself, which I know will only produce worry and anxiety in the long run. I can depend on You, and I choose to accept every good and perfect gift You desire to bring my way. I thank You in Jesus' name. Amen.*

## Next Steps

*Which Bible passage mentioned in this chapter feels most meaningful to you as an expression of God's promise to provide for your needs? Write out that passage in the space below.*

_____

_____

_____

_____

_____

_____

_____

_____

_____

_____

_____

_____

_____

*What step can you take this week to receive God's promise of provision?*

_____

_____

_____

_____

_____

_____

_____

_____

_____

_____

_____

_____

_____

_____

_____

_____

_____

_____

# CHAPTER TWO

# GOD PROMISES YOU
# FORGIVENESS

*He shall bring forth your righteousness as the light,*
*And your justice as the noonday.*

Psalm 37:6

NOT EVERYONE GROWING UP IN THE 1960S WAS A baseball fan, but everyone knew about Mickey Mantle. His all-American smile appeared regularly on the covers of popular magazines, and everyone talked of his eye-popping home runs, his team spirit, his World Series victories, and the wholesome image he presented to the world. Newspapers worked his name into the headlines—and not just on the sports pages. His friendly, optimistic voice was soothing in a world of Cold War tensions.

Behind the smile, the truth was different. Mantle was a troubled man, severely addicted to alcohol. He was often drunk when he played for the Yankees, and his teammates were amazed that he could hit the ball and run around the bases while inebriated. His family life was a sham, his language was crude and filthy, and he was a serial womanizer who neglected his wife and sons.

In the end, it all caught up to him in the form of a fatal disease. In his final months, Mickey Mantle began looking for forgiveness. He asked forgiveness from his family and apologized to his fans in television interviews. "I'm gonna die," he said. "I've led a terrible life. I've done too many bad things."[1] In his last press conference, he spoke of a lifetime of regrets and eternal hell, a life squandered, and he had this message for the schoolchildren of the world: "Don't be like me."[2]

To everyone's surprise, Mantle began going to church and reaching out to the Lord. Friends like baseball legend Bobby Richardson witnessed to him, and Mickey Mantle reportedly invited Jesus Christ to become his Savior. His heart became tender and responsive to spiritual things. His friend Roy True later said, "When Bobby Richardson came to Mickey and said, 'You're dying, here is a way to make peace,' he embraced it. He wanted to be forgiven."[3]

At the end of Mantle's life, none of the statistics mattered. His fame offered no comfort. His wealth was worthless, his trophies useless. Mickey Mantle just wanted to be forgiven.

At the end of
Mantle's life, none
of the statistics
mattered. His
fame offered no
comfort. His wealth
was worthless, his
trophies useless.
Mickey Mantle
just wanted to
be forgiven.

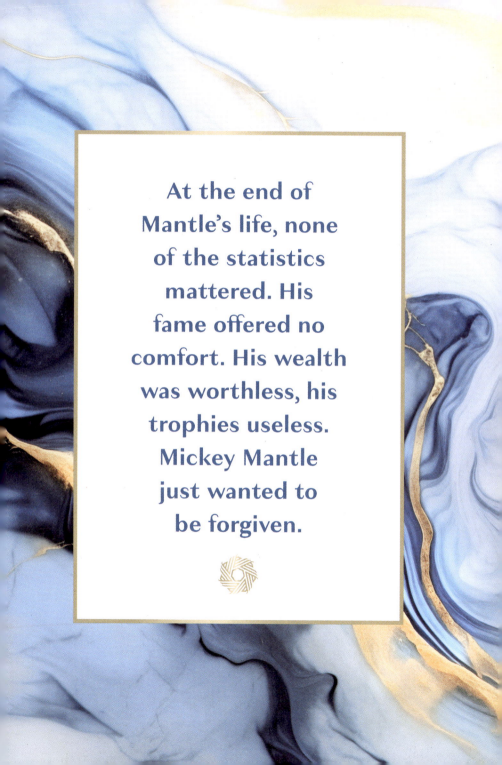

David understood the incredible power of God's forgiveness. He also understood our deep need to experience that forgiveness in our lives, as we can see in Psalm 37.

> Commit your way to the LORD,
> Trust also in Him,
> And He shall bring it to pass.
> He shall bring forth your righteousness as
>     the light,
> And your justice as the noonday. (vv. 5–6)

God "shall bring forth your righteousness as the light." There's a paradox buried in that promise, because you and I don't have any righteousness. Not on our own. We have unrighteousness. Scripture tells us, "There is none righteous, no, not one; there is none who understands. . . . For all have sinned and fall short of the glory of God" (Romans 3:10–11, 23).

We don't have the capacity to generate righteousness within ourselves—which is a problem because righteousness is the key card that grants access to God's kingdom. There are no unrighteous people in heaven.

How, then, do we become righteous? Through faith. When we trust God to forgive our sin, He takes it from us. He removes the stain of our sin and fills us with the righteousness of Jesus. Because of His forgiveness and His righteousness, we are declared not guilty by our holy Judge.

Let's take a deeper look at God's promise of forgiveness—including other ways that promise is expressed in God's Word and how we can apply that forgiveness in our own lives.

## Recognizing God's Promise of Forgiveness

What does it mean to be forgiven by God? Most of us think of forgiveness as a spiritual matter, and there's certainly good reason for viewing it that way. As we've already seen, forgiveness is central to several important spiritual themes—including sin and salvation. God's forgiveness is our key to eternal life.

But the Bible also describes forgiveness as a *legal* issue. *Forgiveness* is a judicial term. Jesus made that clear in a story we often describe as the parable of the unforgiving servant:

> "Therefore the kingdom of heaven is like a certain king who wanted to settle accounts with his servants. And when he had begun to settle accounts, one was brought to him who owed him ten thousand talents. But as he was not able to pay, his

master commanded that he be sold, with his wife and children and all that he had, and that payment be made. The servant therefore fell down before him, saying, 'Master, have patience with me, and I will pay you all.' Then the master of that servant was moved with compassion, released him, and forgave him the debt." (Matthew 18:23–27)

The key to understanding this parable is understanding the debt owed by the servant in question. When we read "ten thousand talents," we might think of a large financial sum. Maybe "ten thousand dollars," or even ten thousand days' worth of wages.

But no. In the ancient world, a "talent" was a measure of weight that represented the largest possible denomination of currency. If we were to think of a similar concept in today's world, we might describe a talent as a "vault" or a "mint." In Jesus' day, a single talent was far more wealth than any common laborer would ever hope to see in his entire lifetime. And this servant owed a debt of ten thousand talents.

If we were to translate Jesus' parable into the common language of today, we might rephrase that verse like this: "And when he had begun to settle accounts, one was brought to him who owed him $10 billion." That's the idea conveyed by Christ in this story. The servant's debt was an unfathomable amount. It was an insurmountable obstacle standing between the servant and his personal freedom.

Now, with that information fresh in your mind, imagine the shock Jesus' listeners would have experienced when He said these words: "Then the master of that servant was moved with compassion, released him, and forgave him the debt."

That's what it means to be forgiven by God: "released." The weight of our sin is removed. The legal pressure of the debt we owe to God is taken away.

For those of us who were alive during the 1970s, the Watergate scandal remains a seminal event in our nation's history. For the first and only time, a United States president was forced to resign his office and step away from the White House. The entire nation was gripped by the scandal, which threatened to tear apart some of our most important institutions. It was a season of strife, derision, and division.

Gerald Ford became president after the resignation of Richard Nixon, and it fell to Ford to find a solution to the disunity of the United States—to find a way for all involved to move forward toward a better tomorrow. Ford's solution was controversial at the time but has since been largely vindicated by history. He chose forgiveness.

That's what it means
to be forgiven by
God: "released."
The weight of our
sin is removed. The
legal pressure of
the debt we owe to
God is taken away.

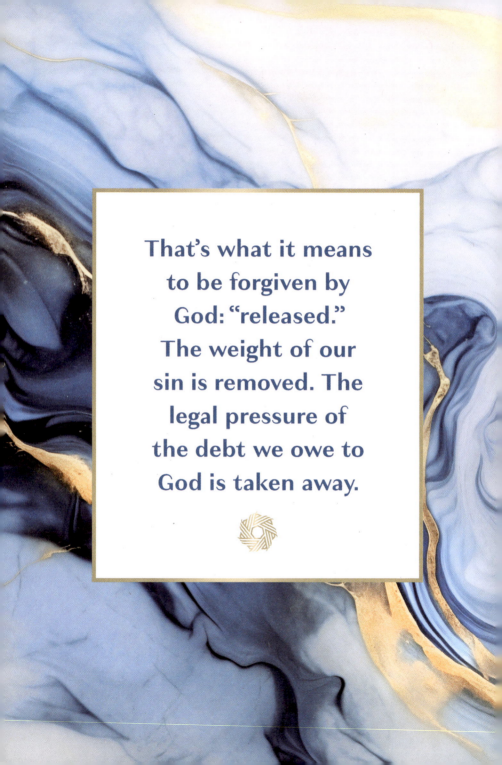

Speaking from the Oval Office on September 8, 1974, Ford made a startling proclamation:

> I, Gerald R. Ford, president of the United States, pursuant to the pardon power conferred upon me by Article II, Section 2, of the Constitution, have granted and by these presents do grant a full, free, and absolute pardon unto Richard Nixon for all offenses against the United States which he, Richard Nixon, has committed or may have committed or taken part in during the period from January 20, 1969 through August 9, 1974.[4]

That's also what it means to receive forgiveness from God. He grants a "full, free, and absolute pardon" to you and me for every sin and offense committed against Him during our lifetimes. The debt of that sin is insurmountable, but God removes it. Completely. He pardons us in a legal sense, meaning every wrong we have committed or will ever commit is purged from our permanent record.

Several passages in God's Word describe this legal process of forgiveness in different ways. Here are a few meaningful examples:

- "'Come now, and let us reason together,' says the LORD, 'though your sins are like scarlet, they shall be as white as snow; though they are red like crimson, they shall be as wool'" (Isaiah 1:18).

- "Who is a God like You, pardoning iniquity and passing over the transgression of the remnant of His heritage? He does not retain His anger forever, because He delights in mercy. He will again have compassion on us, and will subdue our iniquities. You will cast all our sins into the depths of the sea" (Micah 7:18–19).
- "He has delivered us from the power of darkness and conveyed us into the kingdom of the Son of His love, in whom we have redemption through His blood, the forgiveness of sins" (Colossians 1:13–14).

Now, there's one more important point we need to address about God's promise of forgiveness. Namely, that our acceptance of that promise requires us to forgive as well. Not to forgive God, of course, but to forgive other people—those who have wronged us or hurt us.

Consider these sober words from Jesus: "For if you forgive men their trespasses, your heavenly Father will also forgive you. But if you do not forgive men their trespasses, neither will your Father forgive your trespasses" (Matthew 6:14–15).

Note the principle here: To be forgiven, we must be willing to forgive. Or, to say it in reverse, we cannot experience the full power of God's forgiveness in our lives if we are unwilling to extend that power over the lives of others. That's what Jesus was communicating in His parable of the unforgiving servant. Consider the end of the story:

"But that servant went out and found one of his fellow servants who owed him a hundred denarii; and he laid hands on him and took him by the throat, saying, 'Pay me what you owe!' So his fellow servant fell down at his feet and begged him, saying, 'Have patience with me, and I will pay you all.' And he would not, but went and threw him into prison till he should pay the debt. So when his fellow servants saw what had been done, they were very grieved, and came and told their master all that had been done. Then his master, after he had called him, said to him, 'You wicked servant! I forgave you all that debt because you begged me. Should you not also have had compassion on your fellow servant, just as I had pity on you?' And his master was angry, and delivered him to the torturers until he should pay all that was due to him. So My heavenly Father also will do to you if each of you, from his heart, does not forgive his brother his trespasses." (Matthew 18:28–35)

> **Forgiveness is available now, and forgiven sins are never again remembered. They fall into the never-ending ocean of grace and will never be recalled.**

## Receiving God's Promise of Forgiveness

Every human instinctively wants to be forgiven. We don't want to walk around marked by our mistakes; we want our sins washed away. Only a merciful God can do that, and He does it only through the blood of Jesus Christ, His Son. Ephesians 1:7 says, "In [Christ] we have redemption through His blood, the forgiveness of sins, according to the riches of His grace."

Forgiveness is available now, and forgiven sins are never again remembered. They fall into the never-ending ocean of grace and will never be recalled. The Bible says, "For You, Lord, are good, and ready to forgive, and abundant in mercy to all those who call upon You. . . . There is forgiveness with You, that You may be feared" (Psalms 86:5; 130:4).

Here's something I've noticed during my years as a pastor: Many Christians know these promises without really experiencing them—without *feeling* forgiven. There is a disconnect between what they believe and what they feel.

If you're struggling with *being* forgiven or with *feeling* forgiven, I suggest three things to help you receive this important promise from your heavenly Father.

*Confess.* First, confess your sins to God. Tell Him you're willing to turn away from those sins. With His grace you can change your thoughts and habits. "If we confess our sins, He is faithful and just to forgive us our sins and to cleanse us from all unrighteousness" (1 John 1:9).

To truly experience forgiveness, we must acknowledge our sinfulness before God in earnest prayer. We tell Him we're sorry, ask His forgiveness, tell Him we're willing to turn from sin, and then trust Him to be faithful to forgive our sin and to cleanse our hearts.

You can do this today in a definite way. If you've never asked Jesus to come into your life, you can bow your head now, confess your sins, and turn your life over to Him. If you're a Christian who still struggles with guilt, you can come before the Lord in an act of prayer and once and forever confess the sins or transgressions that are haunting you, reassuring yourself that they're nailed to the cross of Christ for all time and eternity.

*Claim.* Second, by faith claim God's promises about forgiveness. We've already covered several of those promises, but there are more. For example, Hebrews 10:17 says, "Their sins and their lawless deeds I will remember no more." That is a promise from God, the creator and sustainer of the universe. He will keep that promise, which means you and I can claim it as absolute truth.

We often say that God *forgives* and *forgets* our sins, but we may wonder whether that's really the case. How can God, who is all-knowing, forget anything? When we commit a sin against Him, it's a deed done in time and space. It is a historical event. It's something that really happened. If God were to forget an event in history, He would no longer be all-knowing; and if He isn't omniscient, how can He be God?

I think the concept of our sins being "forgotten" is true in a judicial sense. Remember, forgiveness is a legal proceeding. The passage in Hebrews 10 describes the ministry of Jesus Christ as our Great High Priest. The sacrifice He made was once and for all. Because of Christ's blood, God expunges the record of our sins. No other sacrifice is ever again needed. No record of our sins remains on heaven's books—not a dash, not a comma, not a smudge. Though God omnisciently knows everything that has ever happened or will ever happen, He will never again view us with that sin in mind. It's as though it never occurred.

*Conceptualize.* Third, when we confess our sins and claim God's promises regarding forgiveness, we can use biblical imagery to break the shackles of shame that linger in our hearts.

The Bible says, for example, "As far as the east is from the west, so far has He removed our transgressions from us" (Psalm 103:12). Take a moment to meditate on that verse, picturing it in your mind until it settles down in your soul. Visualize the sin that makes you feel ashamed—the mistakes that have haunted your past and placed a pall on your future. Now visualize God reaching down and separating you from that sin. Completely. Totally. It's gone.

The Bible is full of such images. Isaiah 55:7 uses the wonderful phrase "He will abundantly pardon." Colossians 2:13–14 says, "He has . . . forgiven you all trespasses, having wiped out the handwriting of requirements that was against us . . . having nailed it to the cross." Isaiah 43:25 tells us God has blotted out our sins.

Memorize some of these verses and quote them when the devil accuses your heart. Conceptualize the

Visualize the sin
that makes you
feel ashamed—
the mistakes that
have haunted your
past and placed a
pall on your future.
Now visualize God
reaching down and
separating you from
that sin. Completely.
Totally. It's gone.

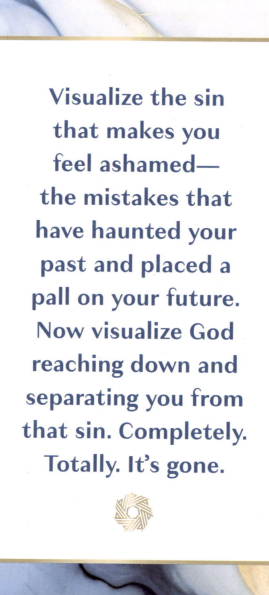

images God provides. Practice meditating on God's casting your sins as far from you as east is from west, of their being wiped out, blotted out, on being abundantly pardoned.

When God forgives our sins, they're never thought of or brought up again, never dredged up, and never held against us. When you come to Him in contrite confession, you can trust Him to nail your sins to the cross of Christ, to cover them with His blood, to blot them out of His book, to abundantly pardon, to wash you whiter than snow, to cast your sins behind His back, to cast them into the depths of the sea, to remove them as far as the east is from the west, and to remember them no more.

David recorded that kind of conceptualization in Psalm 51 after sinning publicly by forcing a sexual encounter with Bathsheba and subsequently having her husband murdered. David understood the weight of his sin, but he also understood the power and completeness of God's forgiveness.

Listen to how David incorporated that forgiveness into his life:

> Have mercy upon me, O God,
> According to Your lovingkindness;
> According to the multitude of Your tender
>      mercies,
> Blot out my transgressions.

Wash me thoroughly from my iniquity,
And cleanse me from my sin.

For I acknowledge my transgressions,
And my sin is always before me.
Against You, You only, have I sinned,
And done this evil in Your sight—
That You may be found just when You speak,
And blameless when You judge. . . .

Purge me with hyssop, and I shall be clean;
Wash me, and I shall be whiter than snow.
Make me hear joy and gladness,
That the bones You have broken may
    rejoice.
Hide Your face from my sins,
And blot out all my iniquities.
    (Psalm 51:1–4, 7–9)

As a firefighter and EMT, Matt Swatzell was used to long days at work. But after a twenty-four-hour shift doing his best to serve the community, Matt fell asleep behind the wheel while driving home. In that moment of unconsciousness, he struck another car about four miles from his home. June Fitzgerald was driving that car; she was pregnant, and her young daughter was strapped in the back seat.

Tragically, both June and her unborn child were killed in the crash. The little girl, whose name is Faith, survived.

Obviously, Matt Swatzell was distraught about the outcome of his failure. So was June's husband, Erik Fitzgerald. Erik was a pastor who had preached on the topic of forgiveness many times. Now, forced to confront the tragic death of his wife and unborn child, he saw an opportunity to put forgiveness into practice.

To start, Erik entered a plea during Matt's trial to ask for leniency in the sentencing. Then, once the trial was over, Erik began meeting with Matt twice a week. He chose to disciple the man responsible for the greatest loss in his life.

"You forgive as you've been forgiven," Erik told reporters, referencing Jesus' words from Matthew 6. "It wasn't an option. If you've been forgiven, then you need to extend that forgiveness."[5]

The story of Erik Fitzgerald and Matt Swatzell is a reflection of what God has promised to all who believe in Him: forgiveness. Your sins are forgiven. Your guilt is removed. Your shame and failure can be removed as well. Choose to accept and embrace the wonderful gift of God's full, free, and final pardon.

*Heavenly Father, as David prayed, please have mercy on me. I choose to confess my sin rather than hide it. I choose to claim Your forgiveness rather than try to justify myself or my actions. I choose to be grateful for Your grace and mercy, which You have poured over me throughout all my life. Thank You, Father, in Jesus' name. Amen.*

## Next Steps

*Which Bible passage mentioned in this chapter feels most meaningful to you as an expression of God's promise of forgiveness? Write out that passage in the space below.*

_____

_____

_____

_____

_____

_____

_____

_____

_____

_____

_____

_____

*What step can you take this week to receive*
*God's promise of forgiveness?*

_____

_____

_____

_____

_____

_____

_____

_____

_____

_____

_____

_____

_____

_____

_____

_____

_____

_____

# CHAPTER THREE

# GOD PROMISES YOU
# PEACE

*Rest in the LORD, and wait patiently for Him;*
*Do not fret because of him who prospers in his way,*
*Because of the man who brings wicked schemes to pass.*

Psalm 37:7

WHEN A SERIES OF WILDFIRES THREATENED THE SMALL town of Lake Arrowhead, California, in September 2024, Dayna Wyland prepared to evacuate her home and community. Wyland tried to stay and ride out the flames but ultimately packed her bags when she received a third emergency alert on her phone.

"My car is full of pictures because I'm so sentimental," she told reporters. "That's what's important to me, pictures. My car [is] full of pictures [from] all over the house. Photo albums, everything."

Normally, a family evacuating because of wildfires would not be a newsworthy story. I myself have been forced to evacuate because of fires on more than one occasion. But Dayna Wyland's story is different because this was not the first time she'd fled from the wrath of nature. Or the second. Or the third.

Incredibly, Dayna Wyland has experienced (and survived) five natural disasters over the course of her lifetime. The first was Hurricane Katrina in 2005, when Wyland's home was submerged. Her family jumped in their car just in time and drove across the border into Texas. Then, only a few months later, they were forced to evacuate again when Hurricane Rita slammed into the Gulf Coast. A few years after that, the Wylands evacuated their new home because of wildfires. Then, in 2022, they were trapped inside their home for eleven days without power because of a blizzard. Two years after that came the second wildfire evacuation in Lake Arrowhead.

After her fifth natural disaster, Dayna Wyland was christened by many on the internet as the "world's unluckiest woman." Her son recently tried to convince her to move closer to him in Pittsburgh, where there are relatively few natural disasters—but she wasn't convinced, saying, "I said I'm sure I'll bring one with me, like flooding or something."[1]

Now, we don't all face a cluster of natural disasters that send us running from our homes—thank goodness! But we do all face stress. We all face seasons in which we feel like we're buried by so much stress that we'll never make it through.

That's important because stress is a killer. It contributes to high blood pressure, heart disease, and addictive disorders. It often leads to headaches and backaches. It results in trembling of the hands and fingers, lightheadedness, ringing in the ears, cold hands, and dry mouth. It can dramatically affect the skin by triggering psoriasis, eczema, hives, and itching. It has been traced to stomach and breathing disorders. Stress can cause hair loss, mood swings, insomnia, and nightmares. It produces nervous habits in the body like fidgeting of feet and finger tapping. People under stress often lose energy and struggle with chronic fatigue. They're apt to gain or lose weight, and many researchers believe that stress can trigger life-threatening diseases such as cancer, strokes, and heart attacks.

That's just a partial list.

Christians certainly aren't immune to stress. The Bible shares stories of men and women who dealt with high levels of pressure. The apostle Paul told the Corinthians,

We do not want you to be uninformed, brothers and sisters, about the troubles we experienced in the province of Asia. We were under great pressure, far beyond our ability to endure, so that we despaired of life itself. Indeed, we felt we had received the sentence of death. But this happened that we might not rely on ourselves but on God, who raises the dead. (2 Corinthians 1:8–9 NIV)

> **Christians certainly aren't immune to stress. The Bible shares stories of men and women who dealt with high levels of pressure.**

David also understood the crushing pressures connected with stress. After his victory over Goliath, he achieved great success as a soldier and captain in King Saul's army. Then he became an object of jealousy and attempted murder. For years Saul hunted David across the wilderness, forcing him to live in caves and remain on the run. When Saul finally died and David became king, he took on the burden of leadership for a large and expanding nation—including spiritual leadership. And because of his sins against Bathsheba and Uriah, the later years of David's life were filled with familial strife, including his own son attempting to kill him and seize the throne.

So yes, David struggled with stress. And in the midst of that struggle, he learned how to find what all of us need in such seasons: the promise of God's peace and rest.

Let's look again at David's words from Psalm 37:

> Rest in the LORD, and wait patiently
>      for Him;
> Do not fret because of him who prospers in
>      his way,
> Because of the man who brings wicked
>      schemes to pass.
> Cease from anger, and forsake wrath;
> Do not fret—it only causes harm. (vv. 7–8)

A little later in that psalm, David spoke more directly of peace as a promise from God: "But the meek shall inherit the earth, and shall delight themselves in the abundance of peace" (v. 11).

The bad news is this: We're all going to experience

stress in this life. Lots of stress. But here's the good news: God promises to fill us with peace—an abundance of His peace—that will carry us through even the worst of situations. Let's learn a little more about how that process works.

## Recognizing God's Promise of Peace

Have you heard of the "Sunday scaries"? It's a relatively new term that describes the stress many people experience on Sunday afternoons when they start thinking about everything they need to handle or accomplish once the work (or school) week begins.

According to a recent poll, 49 percent of adults are burdened with feelings of anxiety or dread on Sunday because of what they know will be waiting for them come Monday morning. These feelings of trepidation typically start to set in somewhere around 4:00 p.m., and they often ruin the rest of Sunday afternoon and evening. What's more, a typical adult in America today can expect to deal with the Sunday scaries thirty-six times every year. That's nine months' worth of Sundays bogged down by anxiety and stress![2]

As followers of Jesus, we are called to something far greater than the Sunday scaries. We are called to fill ourselves with God's peace. That is a call and a

As followers of Jesus,
we are called to
something far greater
than the Sunday
scaries. We are called
to fill ourselves
with God's peace.

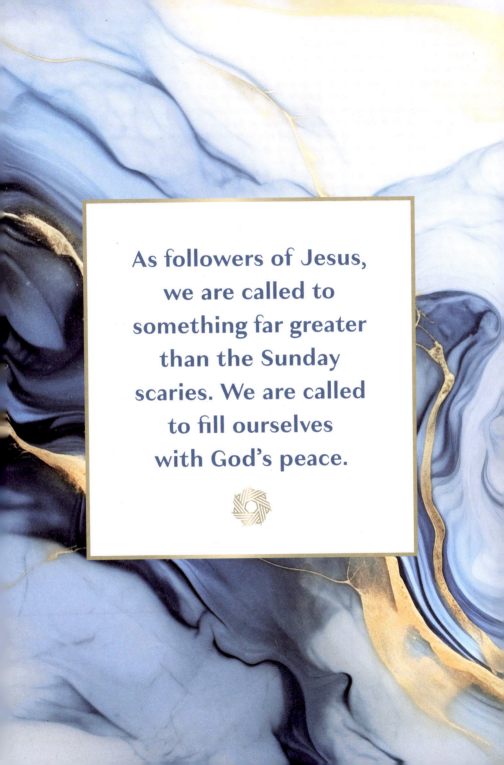

promise emphasized over and over within the pages of God's Word.

Perhaps the most beautiful iteration of God's promise to fill us with peace is found in Paul's letter to the church at Philippi. He wrote,

> Be anxious for nothing, but in everything by prayer and supplication, with thanksgiving, let your requests be made known to God; and the peace of God, which surpasses all understanding, will guard your hearts and minds through Christ Jesus. (Philippians 4:6–7)

Now that's a promise!

Notice, however, that the promise is preceded by two commands: First, "Be anxious for nothing." And second, "In everything by prayer and supplication, with thanksgiving, let your requests be made known to God."

To experience the blessing of God's peace, then, we must first close the door on anxiety. On worry. That doesn't mean we'll never experience those emotions, but it does mean we don't allow ourselves to become overwhelmed by them. Instead, when anxiety and worry and stress begin to press against our hearts and minds, we must quickly pivot to that second command, which is prayer. We release our stress and strain by casting ourselves at the feet of our Savior—and by doing so with a mindset of thanksgiving for all He has already provided for us.

When that happens, we will experience a peace so powerful that it "surpasses all understanding." A peace that applies not just to our hearts (our emotions) but also to our minds. To our thoughts. God's peace.

Jesus also promised to provide us with peace. Actually, He made that promise on several occasions throughout the Gospels, including these:

- "Come to Me, all you who labor and are heavy laden, and I will give you rest. Take My yoke upon you and learn from Me, for I am gentle and lowly in heart, and you will find rest for your souls. For My yoke is easy and My burden is light" (Matthew 11:28–30).
- "Peace I leave with you, My peace I give to you; not as the world gives do I give to you. Let not your heart be troubled, neither let it be afraid" (John 14:27).
- "These things I have spoken to you, that in Me you may have peace. In the world you will have tribulation; but be of good cheer, I have overcome the world" (John 16:33).

Actually, something interesting happens throughout the Gospels when we focus on Jesus and the promise of

> **Jesus spoke "peace" to many people He encountered, including those He healed. That word—and that promise—was constantly on His lips.**

peace. Specifically, Jesus spoke "peace" to many people He encountered, including those He healed. That word—and that promise—was constantly on His lips.

For example, when Jesus rebuked the storm on the Sea of Galilee, He cried out, "Peace, be still!" (Mark 4:39). When Jesus blessed the sinful woman who washed His feet in Simon's house, He told her, "Your faith has saved you. Go in peace" (Luke 7:50). When He healed the woman with the issue of blood, He told her,

"Daughter, be of good cheer; your faith has made you well. Go in peace" (Luke 8:48). When Jesus gave instructions to His disciples before sending them out to minister, He told them to speak these words whenever they entered someone's home: "Peace to this house" (Luke 10:5). When Jesus appeared to His disciples after the resurrection, the first thing He said to them was "Peace to you" (Luke 24:36). One of the last things He said to those same disciples before He ascended into heaven was "Peace to you! As the Father has sent Me, I also send you" (John 20:21).

Do you see the pattern? Jesus constantly spoke about peace. More than that, He constantly blessed those He encountered by speaking peace over their lives. His peace.

You and I can be beneficiaries of that same blessing—that same promise. We have unlimited access to God's unending peace.

## Receiving God's Promise of Peace

We saw in the previous section that children of God have a role to play in receiving His promise of peace. Namely, He has commanded us to turn away from anxiety and stress, and He has commanded us to turn toward Him through prayer. When we obey those steps, we open ourselves to receive His promise of peace.

So let's take a closer look at this process of receiving

God's peace. I want to offer three steps you can take to prepare yourself so that you can respond well during seasons of stress. You might think of these steps as creating a spiritual emergency kit for your mind and heart—one that is filled not with bandages and medications but with the implements that help us accept and experience God's peace.

*First, collect promises you can claim.* Scripture is a key foundation for our lives as followers of Jesus, and Scripture also serves as the primary ingredient for our spiritual emergency kit.

When Solomon's son Rehoboam ascended the throne, he began thinking in terms of emergency preparedness. With his father dead, Rehoboam expected attacks from neighboring enemies, and he wanted to be prepared. "He fortified the strongholds, and put captains in them, and stores of food, oil, and wine. Also in every city he put shields and spears, and made them very strong" (2 Chronicles 11:11–12).

We, too, should expect attacks from the Enemy, and we need to store up Scriptures as shields for our minds and hearts. Proverbs 10:14 says, "Wise people store up knowledge." And the knowledge we need to deal with seasons of stress and anxiety is knowledge of God's promises. Clinging to those promises will help fill us with peace.

Thankfully, you're in the middle of a book about

We, too, should expect attacks from the Enemy, and we need to store up Scriptures as shields for our minds and hearts.

God's promises, which means you have a great head start on this step! We've already explored several promises, and we have several more yet to go. So grab hold of those promises in a real and tangible way—one that will help you incorporate them in your life. Write them down. Memorize them. Set up reminders on your phone or your calendar. Do whatever it takes for you to surround yourself with God's promises *before* you need to access them. Keep them fully stocked in your spiritual emergency kit.

My friend and fellow pastor Ed Dobson passed away several years back because of ALS (amyotrophic lateral sclerosis). He left behind a little book titled *Prayers and Promises When Facing a Life-Threatening Illness*, in which he described the weakness he felt during his illness. For years he had bored into God's Word like a drill, but now, he said, he found it difficult to read the Bible or even pray. "I could take spiritual truth only in small bites."

Thankfully, God gave him a few verses every day that kept him calm and strong, and many of the verses were ones he had previously stored away in the armory of his mind. One of the passages, Hebrews 13:5–6, helped him more than any other passage in the entire Bible: "He Himself has said, 'I will never leave you nor forsake you.' So we may boldly say: 'The LORD is my helper; I will not fear. What can man do to me?'"

"Soon after my diagnosis," Dobson wrote, "I learned to take five-minute time-outs. Whenever fear would begin taking over my life, I would take a time-out and repeat the verses from Hebrews 13. . . . I would say these words over and over for the entire five minutes. . . . I wrote these verses on a three-by-five card and placed the card on the mirror by my bed. They are the first words I look at every morning when I get up, and they are the last words I look at when I go to bed."[3]

In dealing with his terminal illness, what if Dobson's emergency kit had been empty? What if he hadn't stored away Scripture like a miser hoarding coins? Could he have staved off the anxiety and fear of a terminal disease? I doubt it. Thankfully, Ed's mind was rich with God's Word, and his awareness of God's promises made all the difference.

In a similar way, I encourage you to read, study, learn, memorize, and meditate on God's Word day and night. The Lord will give you verses to store away in your mental silo like Joseph's grain for times of famine.

*Second, collect blessings you can count.* As you read the book of Psalms, you may notice how many psalms were written during crises. This is especially true for David, who—as we've already seen—encountered one difficult circumstance after another throughout his life. Some of David's psalms were written in times of grief, fear, anguish, and desperation.

But David also knew how to count his blessings, and he gave us a prime example in Psalm 103: "Bless the

Just like David, if we cultivate the habit of gratitude and learn to thank God spontaneously throughout the day, we'll have an invaluable skill in our spiritual emergency kit.

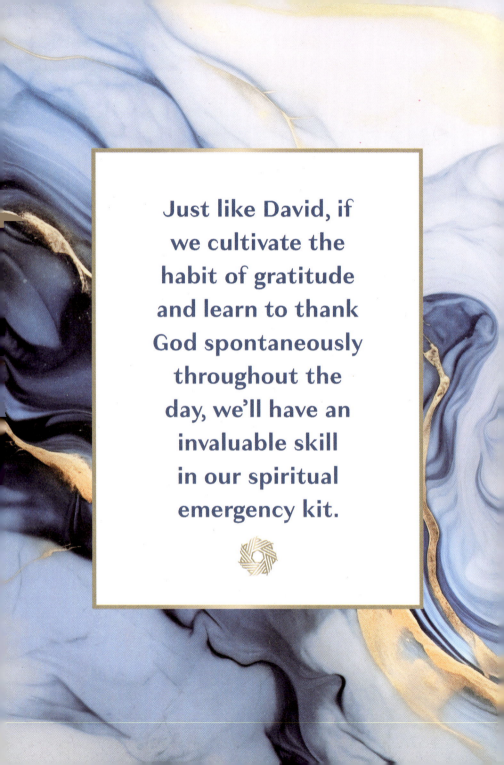

LORD, O my soul; and all that is within me, bless His holy name!" (v. 1). If you read the entire psalm, you will find that every verse is positive in tone. Every line conveys an atmosphere of gratitude to God, who floods our lives with benefits, forgives our iniquities, heals our problems, redeems us from destruction, and crowns us with loving-kindness and tender mercy.

Just like David, if we cultivate the habit of gratitude and learn to thank God spontaneously throughout the day, we'll have an invaluable skill in our spiritual emergency kit. Practically, this means keeping a record of the ways in which God has blessed you in the past and also keeping an eye out for the blessings (big and small) He provides for you each day.

In short, count your blessings. Doing so regularly will supercharge your ability to receive God's promised peace.

*Third, collect attitudes you can cultivate.* In the same way we fill our spiritual emergency kit with an understanding of God's promises and an awareness of His blessings, we can store up within ourselves the kind of attitudes that honor Him—and that help us receive His promise of peace.

For example, the Bible teaches that faith, trust, assurance, confidence, and calmness are God-pleasing virtues. Contrary to what many think, such virtues are not based on genetics or DNA; they are available to all people—including you and me.

Here are just a few of the godly attitudes that fill the pages of Scripture:

- "Be careful, keep calm and don't be afraid. Do not lose heart" (Isaiah 7:4 NIV).
- "A man of understanding is of a calm spirit" (Proverbs 17:27).
- "Now may the God of hope fill you with all joy and peace in believing, that you may abound in hope by the power of the Holy Spirit" (Romans 15:13).
- "Therefore, as the elect of God, holy and beloved, put on tender mercies, kindness, humility, meekness, longsuffering; bearing with one another, and forgiving one another, if anyone has a complaint against another; even as Christ forgave you, so you also must do" (Colossians 3:12–13).
- "But also for this very reason, giving all diligence, add to your faith virtue, to virtue knowledge, to knowledge self-control, to self-control perseverance, to perseverance godliness, to godliness brotherly kindness, and to brotherly kindness love" (2 Peter 1:5–7).

Christians, more than anyone, should be people of understanding—people who cultivate calm, confident spirits. We are related by the new birth to the God who controls all events, who knows the end from the beginning, who knows all that happens before it occurs. We've placed our faith in a King who causes all things to work together for the good of those who love Him. We have instant access to the throne of grace, and we know our God is a very present help in trouble—a mighty fortress.

Why, then, are we so prone to panic?

The residents of Mucusso—a town in the African nation of Angola—had reason to panic several years back. The town was home to about four thousand people, all of whom were startled one day to feel a strong, sustained vibration coming up through the ground beneath their feet. Some thought they were experiencing an earthquake, but they were wrong. Minutes later, those same residents heard an ominous roar swell around them. Some thought there must be a thunderstorm approaching, but they were wrong. Then those residents saw a dust cloud rise up into the air outside the town. Some thought a tornado was about to strike, but they were wrong.

What was the cause of these fear-inducing sensations? A herd of elephants. Hundreds of elephants. The wild beasts had stampeded across the border from the nearby nation of Botswana, and they rampaged through Mucusso destroying homes, gardens, farms, and more.[4]

Thankfully, no people were injured. But I certainly wouldn't blame the people of Mucusso for feeling a little on edge after the stampede ended.

I also don't blame you for feeling a little on edge about the stressful situations in your life—both past and present. Your trials and tribulations are real, and they take a real toll on everyone, including followers of Christ. Even so, don't be defined by your stress. Don't settle for a life of worry and anxiety. God has promised to fill you with His peace—a peace that passes all understanding.

*Heavenly Father, I need Your peace today. Burdens are pressing down on me, and fears make me want to shrink back from Your work and Your will. Instead of choosing to be afraid, I will claim Your promise of peace. I will trust You to fill me with Your peace, which passes all understanding. In Jesus' name, amen.*

## Next Steps

*Which Bible passage mentioned in this chapter feels most meaningful to you in connection with God's promise of peace? Write out that passage in the space below.*

_____

_____

_____

_____

_____

_____

_____

_____

_____

_____

_____

*What step can you take this week to receive*
*God's promise of peace?*

_____

_____

_____

_____

_____

_____

_____

_____

_____

_____

_____

_____

_____

_____

_____

_____

_____

# CHAPTER FOUR

# GOD PROMISES YOU
# PROTECTION

*The wicked have drawn the sword*
*And have bent their bow,*
*To cast down the poor and needy,*
*To slay those who are of upright conduct.*
*Their sword shall enter their own heart,*
*And their bows shall be broken.*

Psalm 37:14–15

IN DECEMBER 2024, A MAN NAMED HECTOR Maldonado visited a Walmart superstore in Chesterfield County, Virginia. Many people have a lot of shopping to do at that time of year, but Maldonado entered the store with a different goal in mind: shoplifting. He'd come as a thief intending to steal.

Working from aisle to aisle, Maldonado stuffed his clothing with more than $1,400 worth of merchandise. He was brazen about the theft, not even attempting to hide what he was doing.

There was just one problem: Maldonado engaged his shoplifting spree in the middle of an event called

Shop with a Cop. Every year for several years running, Chesterfield police officers have shown up at local stores to partner with impoverished children. The officers take the children shopping for much-needed Christmas gifts and other items. That is why there were more than fifty police offers present in uniform at the Chesterfield Walmart when Hector Maldonado began his shoplifting extravaganza. "We had 30 to 40 marked patrol cars in the parking lot," said Lieutenant James Lamb of the Chesterfield County Police Department. "When we found his vehicle, it was facing where our cars were parked, so he would have had to see them. It seems it just didn't matter to him."

Once a store employee alerted one of the officers about Maldonado's attempted theft, it took only a few moments for the rest of the cops to put a pause on shopping and form a search. The suspect attempted to escape through the back of the store, but he was quickly apprehended and arrested. Later, police found that Maldonado was a repeat offender with several open warrants for larceny in the same county.[1]

There's a sense of poetic justice to the idea of a criminal committing crimes in the middle of a store packed with police officers. But as silly as it may sound, that scenario points to something all of us long for in our hearts: Justice. Security. Protection.

Despite all the rhetoric about defunding the police,

the vast majority of people understand the value of law enforcement. That's because we understand the reality of evil in this world. We've experienced it! We've witnessed it. We know there are scoundrels out there with malevolent motivations who seek to cause trouble within our communities—individuals and organizations who reject righteousness in favor of greed, corruption, and violence. We rely on law enforcement to protect us from such troublemakers.

In a similar way, Bible readers know we have an enemy, Satan, who "walks about like a roaring lion, seeking whom he may devour" (1 Peter 5:8). Our adversary wants to tear down everything that is good and decent in the world. He wants to destroy not only our goals and our dreams, but our very lives.

Therefore, we need protection. We need the kind of security only God can provide. And wouldn't you know it? He has promised to provide that protection for all His children.

David understood the reality (and the importance) of that promise, which is why he included it in Psalm 37, when he wrote that the sword of the wicked "shall enter their own heart" (v. 15).

Have you felt a sword pointed toward you in different seasons of your life? Are you feeling it now? Discrimination and persecution have been all too common in recent years for those who take a stand on biblical

We need the kind of security only God can provide. And wouldn't you know it? He has promised to provide that protection for all His children.

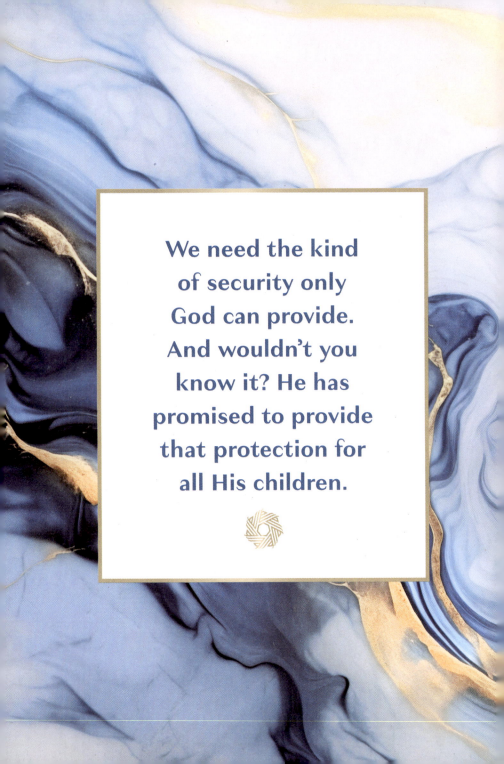

truth. The arrows of physical violence and harassment and intimidation are constantly fired against Christians around the world, especially those who live in nations where they are religious minorities.

Sometimes it feels like we're on our own. Sometimes it seems we have to defend ourselves from the onslaught of evil. Yet even when we feel undefended, we can cling to the truth of Scripture that God stands beside us. Moreover, He stands in front of us as our shield and defender, who breaks the bows of the wicked.

David added these verses a little later in Psalm 37:

> The LORD knows the days of the upright,
> And their inheritance shall be forever.
> They shall not be ashamed in the evil time,
> And in the days of famine they shall be
>     satisfied.
> But the wicked shall perish;
> And the enemies of the LORD,
> Like the splendor of the meadows, shall
>     vanish.
> Into smoke they shall vanish away.
>     (vv. 18–20)

Let's learn more about the specific promises God has made to protect His children both now and into eternity. And as we've done in previous chapters, let's take a closer look at how we can actively receive that promise of protection in our lives.

## Recognizing God's Promise of Protection

The more you read through the Old Testament, the more you realize that the nation of Israel was completely dependent on God's protection. That reality was present at the very beginning, when the descendants of Abraham were rescued by God during the exodus. Egypt was a mighty empire, and the Israelites were slaves. There was nothing God's people could do to free themselves, but God freed them. Then, when Pharaoh changed his mind and decided to pursue the Israelites at the Red Sea, there was again nothing God's people could do to defend themselves—they were trapped between the desert and the sea. But God defended them. He protected them.

What happened next? The Israelites rejected God's command to enter the promised land, which caused them to wander in the wilderness for forty years. Even then, God protected them. He provided for all of their needs. At the end of their sojourn, the Israelites did conquer the promised land under the leadership of Joshua—but the odds were stacked against them. They were fighting a people more fearsome and more numerous than themselves, and yet God's people were victorious. Why? Because God was their sword and their shield.

Over and over throughout the Old Testament, God reached down to protect both the nation of Israel and individual Israelites—people such as Joshua, Gideon, Samson, Saul, David, Elijah, Jonah, and many more. The theme is impossible to miss: God is a guardian of those who love Him and serve Him.

But there's one example of this theme that often gets overlooked, and so I'd like to explore it together in these pages. It's the story of King Hezekiah and his confrontation with Sennacherib, king of Assyria.

After the death of Solomon, the Jewish people split into two kingdoms, the northern kingdom of Israel and the southern kingdom of Judah. Around 720 BC, the armies of Assyria swept out of the north and conquered the northern kingdom of Israel, which had rebelled against God from the time of Solomon's death. Ten tribes of Israel were taken as captives and redistributed throughout the Assyrian Empire.

Then, about twenty years later, an Assyrian king named Sennacherib decided to invade and conquer the southern kingdom of Judah, which contained Jerusalem. At that time, the people of Judah were still attempting to follow God. They made mistakes, but they still desired to live as God's chosen people. So imagine their surprise when the Assyrian army—which numbered in the

> **Over and over throughout the Old Testament, God reached down to protect both the nation of Israel and individual Israelites.... The theme is impossible to miss: God is a guardian of those who love Him and serve Him.**

hundreds of thousands of soldiers—set up a siege against Jerusalem.

On a practical level, the people of Judah had very little chance of survival. They were facing a huge army led by generals and soldiers notorious for their brutality, a veteran army used to waging war and achieving conquests without mercy. In modern-day terms, this would be like Russia invading the tiny nation of Montenegro.

To make matters worse, the king of Assyria sent a letter to Hezekiah, king of Judah, which basically said, "I intend to conquer you, just as I have conquered dozens of other kingdoms. They couldn't stop my armies from rampaging through their lands, and neither can you."

How did Hezekiah respond? The answer is a beautiful picture of approaching God as our shield and protector:

> And Hezekiah received the letter from the hand of the messengers, and read it; and Hezekiah went up to the house of the LORD, and spread it before the LORD. Then Hezekiah prayed before the LORD, and said: "O LORD God of Israel, the One who dwells between the cherubim, You are God, You alone, of all the kingdoms of the earth. You have made heaven and earth. Incline Your ear, O LORD, and hear; open Your eyes, O LORD, and see; and hear the words of Sennacherib, which he has sent to reproach the living God. Truly, LORD, the kings of Assyria have laid waste the nations and their lands, and have cast their gods into the fire; for they were not gods, but the work of men's hands—wood and stone. Therefore they destroyed them. Now therefore, O LORD our God, I pray, save us

from his hand, that all the kingdoms of the earth may know that You are the LORD God, You alone." (2 Kings 19:14–19)

Don't you love the picture of Hezekiah physically bringing the offending letter and spreading it out at the house of the Lord? The king carried his problem to God and said, "This is far too large for me to handle. Please take it. Please protect us."

And God did. He preserved His people:

And it came to pass on a certain night that the angel of the LORD went out, and killed in the camp of the Assyrians one hundred and eighty-five thousand; and when people arose early in the morning, there were the corpses—all dead. So Sennacherib king of Assyria departed and went away, returned home, and remained at Nineveh. Now it came to pass, as he was worshiping in the temple of Nisroch his god, that his sons Adrammelech and Sharezer struck him down with the sword; and they escaped into the land of Ararat. Then Esarhaddon his son reigned in his place. (vv. 35–37)

Do you remember what David wrote in Psalm 37:15? "Their sword shall enter their own heart, and their bows shall be broken." That was true then. It's true now. God protects His people.

Many other biblical passages highlight God's promise to protect His people. Here are just a few examples:

- "He who dwells in the secret place of the Most High shall abide under the shadow of the Almighty. I will say of the LORD, 'He is my refuge and my fortress; my God, in Him I will trust.' Surely He shall deliver you from the snare of the fowler and from the perilous pestilence. He shall cover you with His feathers, and under His wings you shall take refuge; His truth shall be your shield and buckler" (Psalm 91:1–4).
- "The name of the LORD is a strong tower; the righteous run to it and are safe" (Proverbs 18:10).
- "My sheep hear My voice, and I know them, and they follow Me. And I give them eternal life, and they shall never perish; neither shall anyone snatch them out of My hand. My Father, who has given them to Me, is greater than all; and no one is able to snatch them out of My Father's hand" (John 10:27–29).
- "But the Lord is faithful, who will establish you and guard you from the evil one" (2 Thessalonians 3:3).

You might be thinking, *Dr. Jeremiah, aren't there lots of times in the Bible and in history when God didn't protect His people?* The answer is yes—in the short term. Scripture tells us Saul was killed by the Philistines. Jerusalem was eventually conquered by the armies of Babylon (and later by Rome). Stephen was martyred. So were Peter and Paul. Throughout history we've learned the names of many women and men who gave their lives for the cause of Christ, from Perpetua to Nate Saint and beyond.

How should we respond to those realities?

There are times when God allows His children to experience pain and suffering. There are even times when He allows some to be killed because of their faith. In those moments, it may seem as if our adversary has triumphed—but has he? Does Satan win when Christians are killed?

No. The Christians themselves are transported into God's presence, where they enjoy a new level of God's protection. Their souls are shielded, and they reside with God in paradise. And those of us left here on earth get to see another picture of Christ removing the sting of death. We get to see the shining faith of those who were shepherded by Jesus even at the end of their physical lives.

This is why we can say along with the author of Hebrews, "The Lord is my helper; I will not fear. What can man do to me?" (13:6).

# Receiving God's Promise of Protection

Charles Ponzi arrived in the United States from Italy in 1903, sailing into Boston Harbor aboard the *SS Vancouver*. For more than fifteen years, he attempted to make a life as a semi-honest businessman and employee. He worked as a clerk in different shops. He was a musical drummer. He worked in factories. He sold insurance and repaired sewing machines. He even joined his wife's family fruit company.

All of his efforts failed. Sure, they provided a living, but they did not usher Ponzi into the glorious wealth and comfort he had dreamed of when he first set sail for America.

Ponzi's breakthrough finally arrived in 1919 when he discovered the income potential of International Reply Coupons (IRCs). Without getting too technical, IRCs were a kind of postage that could be purchased and redeemed in multiple countries, including throughout Europe and America. Ponzi realized that slight differences in the redemptive value of these IRCs meant they could be purchased in one nation and exchanged in another for a slight profit.

This was the beginning of Ponzi's sinister scheme. Taking out an advertisement in the *Boston Globe*, Ponzi sold promissory notes claiming returns of 50 percent interest after ninety days. He sold investors on the notion

Our culture even tries to sell us on the spiritual Ponzi scheme of good works, claiming that we can feel confident in eternity as long as we do more good things than bad things. As long as we are "good people." Such promises are false.

that he'd set up an elaborate system of agents who purchased IRCs in Europe, which he then sold in America for a tidy profit. In reality Ponzi used the money from new investors to pay off old investors, then siphoned off additional funds for himself.

By the fall of 1920, Ponzi was worth an estimated $15 million.

Of course the scheme quickly collapsed once people began digging into his practices. Ponzi was convicted of several federal crimes and spent many years in jail. Later, he was deported back to Italy, where he eventually died with less than seventy-five dollars to his name.[2]

These days, society is filled with an almost infinite number of scams and false promises, all of which claim to offer protection and security in a world that seems scarier by the day. Our culture tells us that financial resources—retirement accounts, savings, investments, and more—will protect us when things go wrong. Our culture tells us that self-help and supportive relationships will provide us with emotional security. Our culture even tries to sell us on the spiritual Ponzi scheme of good works, claiming that we can feel confident in eternity as long as we do more good things than bad things. As long as we are "good people."

Such promises are false. Through no real fault of our own, you and I may lose everything this world has to offer in terms of protection and security. We may lose our financial resources. We may lose our jobs. We may lose our homes. We may lose our closest relationships. We may even lose our health.

Yet none of those things provides true protection or security anyway. None of those things can shield us from the attacks of our adversary who prowls around like a roaring lion seeking those he may devour.

God alone provides protection for our lives and for our souls. Therefore, I encourage you to focus your thoughts and your energy on four realities that no circumstance, locally or globally, can take away from you. These are four elements of your identity that form the basis of your protection under the hand of our loving God.

*First, you are protected by your salvation in Christ.* John 3:16 says that if you have truly believed in the Lord Jesus Christ, then you shall not perish but have everlasting life. As we saw earlier, in John 10:28, Jesus told us that no one—including the devil—can snatch us from the Father's hand once we are saved.

That means you can lose all your money, all your property, all your possessions, but you will never lose your salvation in Jesus Christ.

The apostle Paul phrased it this way:

I am persuaded that neither death nor life, nor angels nor principalities nor powers, nor things present nor things to come, nor height nor depth, nor any other created thing, shall be able to separate us from the love of God which is in Christ Jesus our Lord. (Romans 8:38–39)

*Second, you are protected by the shield of God's promises.* Paul also told us that every believer's faith is a shield that protects them from the Evil One (Ephesians 6:16). Satan speaks lies (John 8:44), but your shield is faith in the truth of God's Word (Psalm 119:160; John 17:17). No angel or human being can take God's truth away from you.

That's why we are spending so much time exploring God's promises in these pages. God has promised you provision. He has promised you forgiveness. He has promised you peace and protection and purpose. He has promised you meaningful connection with Himself, and He has promised you eternal life.

These truths are always true! They will never fail.

*Third, you are protected by your status as a child of God.* One of the ministries performed by the Holy Spirit in you is to testify to you that you are God's child. Not only are you God's child, but your inheritance is already reserved for you in heaven—an inheritance you can never lose.

The Spirit Himself bears witness with our spirit that we are children of God, and if children, then heirs—heirs of God and joint heirs with Christ, if

Satan speaks lies
(John 8:44), but your
shield is faith in the
truth of God's Word
(Psalm 119:160;
John 17:17). No angel
or human being can
take God's truth
away from you.

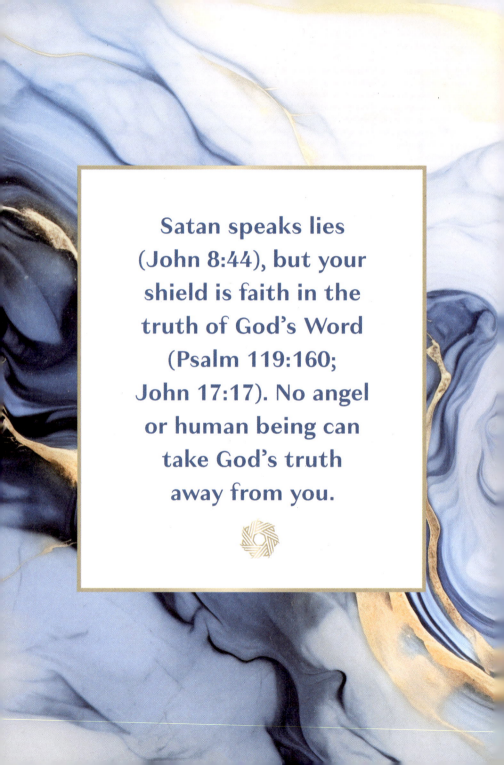

indeed we suffer with Him, that we may also be glorified together. (Romans 8:16–17)

*Fourth, you are protected by soundness of heart and mind.* One of the gifts God has given you is a sound mind with which you are able to counteract the spirit of fear so prevalent in this world. "For God has not given us a spirit of fear, but of power and of love and of a sound mind" (2 Timothy 1:7).

Would God allow anyone to steal from you something He has given you? No. It doesn't matter what else the world may strip away, you and I can choose to stay strong in our minds. We can choose to live under the protection of almighty God.

As we live under the reality of God's protection, let's remain faithful. As Paul wrote to Timothy, let's be "watchful in all things" (2 Timothy 4:5). But there is a difference between watching with confidence and watching from a place of fear and insecurity.

Choose to be confident in God's protection. "Watch, stand fast in the faith, be brave, be strong" (1 Corinthians 16:13).

*Heavenly Father, I believe the stories of protection I read in Your Word. I believe You protected Abraham from his enemies. I believe You protected the Israelites in the wilderness, and I believe You protected David from the pursuit of Saul. I believe You protected the apostle Paul more times than he could remember. And I believe You have been protecting me all of my life. I say yes to Your protection, Lord God. In Jesus' name, amen.*

## Next Steps

*Which Bible passage mentioned in this chapter feels most meaningful to you in connection with God's promise of protection? Write out that passage in the space below.*

_____

_____

_____

_____

_____

_____

_____

_____

_____

_____

_____

*What step can you take this week to receive*
*God's promise of protection?*

_____

_____

_____

_____

_____

_____

_____

_____

_____

_____

_____

_____

_____

_____

_____

_____

_____

# CHAPTER FIVE

# GOD PROMISES YOU
# PURPOSE

*The steps of a good man are ordered by the LORD,*
*And He delights in his way.*
*Though he fall, he shall not be utterly cast down;*
*For the LORD upholds him with His hand.*
Psalm 37:23–24

IN MAY 2022, SANJEEV AND SADHANA PRASAD— natives of India—decided they'd had enough. In their minds, they had been put through emotional turmoil for years. They'd been subjected to mental cruelty and had become laughingstocks in their community. They'd tried to speak with the people harming them, but to no avail. Nothing had come close to solving the problem that was crushing their spirits and darkening their lives.

In desperation, the Prasads decided to seek the only recourse they had left: They sued their own son and daughter-in-law for failing to provide them with grandchildren.

"We are very unhappy," said Mr. Prasad. "We are retired. We want to be grandparents. We are even willing to look after their children. Grandchildren bring joy into people's lives, but we are being deprived of it."

Mrs. Prasad defended the decision to sue: "We had no option but to go to the court. We have been trying to talk to them but whenever we raise the issue of grandchildren, they become evasive. Their decision not to procreate would mean the end of our family name."

Now, suing your own child may seem like taking extreme measures, but the Prasads were comfortable with the decision because of what they perceived as the transactional arrangement between themselves and their offspring. In their minds, they had spent lots of time and money raising their son. More, they had paid for him to attend flight school in America at great expense so that he could become a pilot. After their son returned to India, the Prasads housed him and cared for him while he searched for jobs. They also arranged his marriage to a young woman, which included an extravagant wedding, an expensive honeymoon, and the purchase of a luxury vehicle as a "family car" for the young couple. They had waited six years for their son to start a family, but he refused.

With all that in the background, the Prasads viewed their lawsuit as an ultimatum to their son and daughter-in-law: Give us a grandchild within one year, or pay $650,000.[1]

What should we make of such a case? Is it a comedy or a tragedy? The honest answer is a bit of both. The circumstances feel humorous on the surface, but they point to some deeper longings that have a very real impact on our lives.

At the core, it seems the Prasads and their son were trying to sort through the question of meaning and purpose in their lives. Mr. Prasad himself said he wanted a grandchild because he was seeking "joy." He and his wife were retired, and they sensed a need for something beyond their current experiences—a need for fulfillment. Similarly, their son and his wife seemed to be searching for their own purpose, which at that point focused more on career and fun rather than on raising children.

Let's be clear: Each of us has a longing for purpose. Every person genuinely wants their life to mean something. As a culture, we've developed several terms to describe that longing: *meaning, purpose, significance, fulfillment, satisfaction, validation,* and so on. But no matter what we call it, we all want to believe there's a reason for our existence in the world.

That was certainly true of David, and he wrote about that longing in Psalm 37. He described God's promise to provide meaning and purpose for all who follow Him:

As a culture, we've developed several terms to describe that longing: *meaning, purpose, significance, fulfillment, satisfaction, validation*, and so on. But no matter what we call it, we all want to believe there's a reason for our existence in the world.

> The steps of a good man are ordered by
>     the LORD,
> And He delights in his way.
> Though he fall, he shall not be utterly
>     cast down;
> For the LORD upholds him with His hand.
>     (vv. 23–24)

I wonder how you respond to that first line: "The steps of a good man are ordered by the LORD." Does that sound restrictive? Does it sound as if choosing to follow God means choosing to give up your freedom? Many people make that mistake, but the reality is far more wonderful than we can imagine. Why? Because God's sovereignty is the root of our purpose.

God is the Creator of all things, including our universe and our little planet called Earth. More than that, God is sovereign over all things. He is completely in charge of everything and everyone—including you. The fact that you were born and have a history here on this planet is entirely the result of God's sovereign choice.

Why is that important? Because it means God has a plan for your life. He designed you and fashioned you and planted you within a specific point in time and at a specific geographic location because He has work for you to accomplish. He has a mission for you to fulfill.

That mission is your purpose. And that mission is

> God has a plan for
> your life. He designed
> you and fashioned
> you and planted you
> within a specific
> point in time and at
> a specific geographic
> location because
> He has work for
> you to accomplish.
> He has a mission
> for you to fulfill.

what opens the door for you to be fulfilled. And satisfied. And validated. Your charge from a loving God is what grants you significance.

Let's learn more about these themes together, shall

we? More than that, let's learn about the promises God has made to you—not just to humanity in general but to you specifically—when it comes to finding meaning and purpose in your life.

## Recognizing God's Promise of Purpose

If you've been part of a church body and listened to a fair number of sermons, chances are good you've heard these famous words from Jeremiah 29:11: "'For I know the plans I have for you,' declares the LORD, 'plans to prosper you and not to harm you, plans to give you hope and a future'" (NIV).

Those are wonderful words. Hopeful words. Even healing words. Yet there's controversy in church circles when it comes to who those words were meant for in history and to whom they apply today. Specifically, many preachers or Bible teachers make the case that God was speaking only to the children of Israel when He said those words—not to the rest of us.

Is that true? Let's take a closer look.

The prophet Jeremiah lived and ministered during a particularly difficult season of life for God's chosen people. As I mentioned in chapter 4, the nation of Assyria conquered the northern kingdom of Israel around 720 BC. Jeremiah began his ministry as a prophet about a

hundred years later, and he spoke primarily in the southern kingdom of Judah, which included Jerusalem.

The message Jeremiah preached was not popular,
to say the least. God assigned him to tell the people of
Judah that they also would be conquered. The armies of
Babylon would descend on them, surround Jerusalem,
sack the city, and take captives back to Babylon. Sure
enough, that's exactly what happened. Under King
Nebuchadnezzar, the Babylonians began deporting Jews
from Judah as captives in 597 BC. (The city wasn't
completely conquered until ten years later in 587.)

What we know as Jeremiah 29:11 is actually part of
a letter Jeremiah wrote to the captives living in Babylon
after that first attack. Here's a little more context:

> This is what the LORD says: "When seventy years
> are completed for Babylon, I will come to you and
> fulfill my good promise to bring you back to this
> place. For I know the plans I have for you," declares
> the LORD, "plans to prosper you and not to harm
> you, plans to give you hope and a future. Then you
> will call on me and come and pray to me, and I will
> listen to you. You will seek me and find me when
> you seek me with all your heart." (vv. 10–13 NIV)

So is it true that God was speaking explicitly to the
Jewish captives in Babylon when He declared, "I know

the plans I have for you . . . plans to prosper you and not to harm you"?

Yes, that's true.

Does that mean God doesn't have plans for you and me? Does that mean God hasn't promised a future for you and me—a future that is filled with hope and meaning and purpose and fulfillment?

No. Not at all. I say that for two reasons.

First, God's words are always an outflow of His character. His speech always reflects His values and priorities. So, since God promised to prosper the people of Judah—promised them hope and a future—because they were His children, we know we can count on those same promises now that we have become "children of God" (1 John 3:1). We can trust God to deal with us and care for us as a loving Father, just as He cared for those taken captive to Babylon.

Second, God promised in many other places throughout Scripture that those who follow Him will experience meaning and purpose in their lives. Here are just a few examples:

- "We know that all things work together for good to those who love God, to those who are the called according to His purpose" (Romans 8:28).
- "In Him also we have obtained an inheritance, being predestined according to the purpose

of Him who works all things according to the counsel of His will, that we who first trusted in Christ should be to the praise of His glory" (Ephesians 1:11–12).

- "For we are His workmanship, created in Christ Jesus for good works, which God prepared beforehand that we should walk in them" (Ephesians 2:10).
- "For by Him all things were created that are in heaven and that are on earth, visible and invisible, whether thrones or dominions or principalities or powers. All things were created through Him and for Him. And He is before all things, and in Him all things consist" (Colossians 1:16–17).
- "Therefore do not be ashamed of the testimony of our Lord, nor of me His prisoner, but share with me in the sufferings for the gospel according to the power of God, who has saved us and called us with a holy calling, not according to our works, but according to His own purpose and grace which was given to us in Christ Jesus before time began" (2 Timothy 1:8–9).

You may be thinking, *Dr. Jeremiah, how can I find my purpose?* or *What can I do to experience meaning and fulfillment in my life?*

The answer is for you to look toward your Creator.

We can trust God
to deal with us
and care for us as
a loving Father,
just as He cared
for those taken
captive to Babylon.

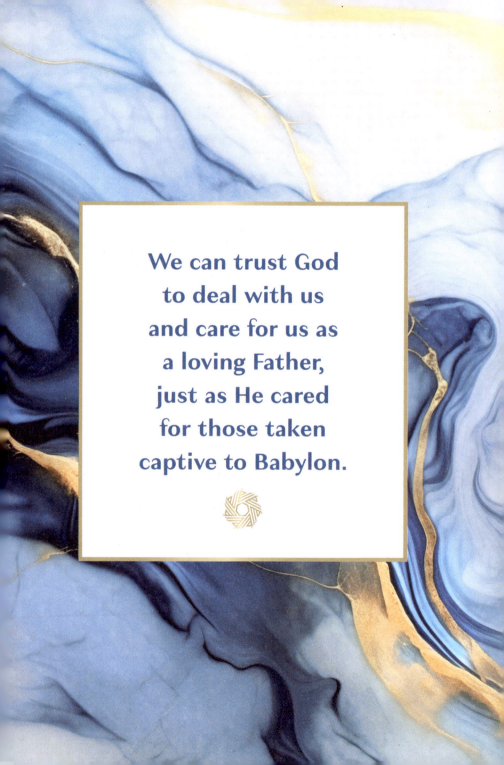

You may not currently understand the plans God has for you, but He does. He created you. He designed you. He made you for a purpose, and you will experience true fulfillment only when you accept that reality and choose to embrace His purpose for your life.

## Receiving God's Promise of Purpose

Here's a driving quiz to set the stage for the second half of this chapter: In which European country does one turn right in order to go left? And in which European country does one turn left in order to go right?

The answer to the first question is France, and the answer to the second is England. The reason for both seeming conundrums is the presence of roundabouts, which are circular intersections in which all the traffic flows in one direction around an island in the middle. Drivers approaching the roundabout from any direction must merge into that flow, circling the island, and then exit onto a new street at the appropriate point. We have relatively few roundabouts in America, but Europe—especially England and France—has tens of thousands of them.

The trick in the questions I asked has to do with which side of the road one drives on. In England, where cars travel on the left side of the street, a driver who wants to turn right at an intersection must first veer left, go clockwise three-quarters of the way around a round-about, then exit in their new direction. Likewise, in France, where cars travel on the right side of the road, a driver approaching an intersection and desiring to turn left must veer right and go counterclockwise around the roundabout before merging onto the new street.

If that sounds confusing, I understand. But round-abouts aren't only for drivers in Europe. We experience them in our lives as well—geographical roundabouts where we try to determine where to live or work, emotional roundabouts where we aren't sure how to feel, and even spiritual roundabouts in which we question our core beliefs.

When we think about meaning and purpose, most of us picture binary choices: We go either this way or that way. Right or left. One direction fits our purpose (or God's purpose), and the other direction moves us away from where we're supposed to be.

Let me ask you, though: Have you found life to be that simple? That easy?

No. Instead, pursuing a life of purpose often leads us straight into a roundabout—a season of spinning in circles as we try to figure out which way to go. Why is that? Why does it so often seem like attempting to follow God's plans for our lives results in confusion, uncertainty, and distress?

To answer that question, let's look more closely at one of the Scripture passages listed previously in this chapter. Most Christians are familiar with Romans 8:28, which says, "We know that all things work together for good to those who love God, to those who are the called according to His purpose." But not as many are as familiar with the context of that verse. Specifically, the word *know* forms a three-step outline in Romans 8 that concludes with verse 28:

- "*We know* that the whole creation groans and labors with birth pangs together until now" (v. 22).
- "We do *not know* what we should pray for" [in the midst of life's "groans and labors"] (v. 26).
- "*We know* that all things work together for good" (v. 28).

Isn't that beautiful? *We know* that life can be difficult. We often *don't know* how to respond or even how to pray. But *we know* that all things—even the difficult things—work together for good to those who love God, to those He has called to fulfill His purpose.

Those verses describe the process of life in a roundabout: scary, difficult, perplexing, and even dangerous! Sometimes we're caught in the flow of life, unable to control what's happening around us while we're carried along by circumstances we are powerless to change. But

> **Why does it so often seem like attempting to follow God's plans for our lives results in confusion, uncertainty, and distress?**

we can know with confidence that God is in control of "all things" in our lives, causing them to work together for our good. The process has lots of moving parts that we don't understand—just like a roundabout—but we *can* understand that God is in control.

See, there is a method to the madness of roundabouts in our lives. As I've said several times in this chapter, God has a purpose for your life—but that purpose involves more than what you do. It involves more than your career

God is using "all things" for His goal of making you more and more like Christ. Accepting that reality is a key step in receiving God's promise of meaning and fulfillment.

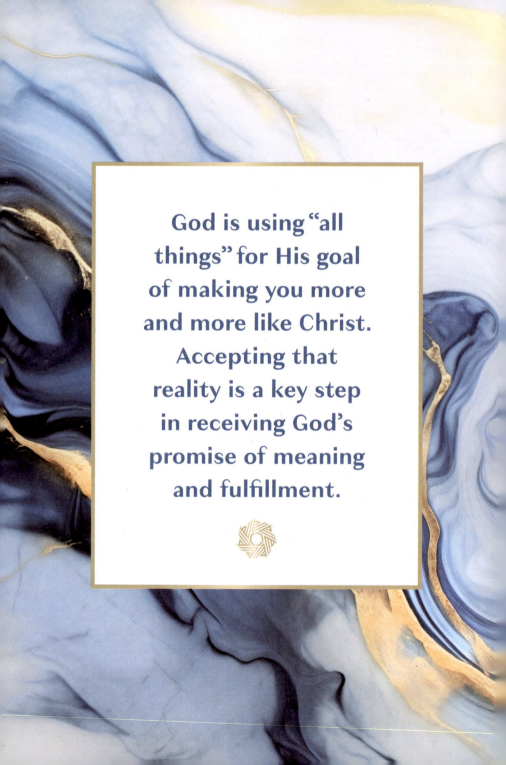

and your family and the different ways you minister within the kingdom of God.

God's purpose also includes *who you are*. And the reason He often sends us on roundabouts is so that He can change who we are into who we need to become. Paul reminded us in Romans 8 that God's purpose is to conform us "to the image of His Son, that [Christ] might be the firstborn among many brethren" (v. 29). Therefore, "all things" (v. 28) in our life are being used by God to get us to the other side of the roundabout—to allow us to exit into eternity in the very image of Jesus Christ. *How* God does it is not always clear. *That* He is doing it is crystal clear from Scripture.

So the next time you find yourself spinning a loop on one of life's roundabouts, don't assume you are outside of God's plan, and don't assume you are missing your purpose. Instead, remember what you can know: God is using "all things" for His goal of making you more and more like Christ. Accepting that reality is a key step in receiving God's promise of meaning and fulfillment.

Looking at more recent history, accepting that reality is what caused Jim Elliot and four other friends to set up a small camp on a sandbar along the Curaray River in Ecuador in 1956. Jim and his friends felt called to share the gospel with a tiny tribe of natives called the Huaorani people, or the "Auca," which means "savage" in their language.

From an outsider's perspective, such a call may have seemed like a roundabout with no end. After all, many Americans in the 1950s couldn't have found Ecuador on a map. And maybe a few dozen people were aware of the existence of the Huaorani people and their minuscule village. Even so, Jim Elliot and his friends were determined to follow what they knew to be God's purpose for their lives. If you've heard the story, you know that Jim and his friends were murdered by the Auca along that riverbank. They were killed as they attempted to share their faith. What kind of purpose could be found in that?

Turns out, a lot. Jim's wife, Elisabeth, and many others not only forgave the Auca natives who killed her husband, but they continued to minister to that tribe—many of whom eventually accepted the lordship of Jesus in their lives.

Despite the hardships and the confusion and the uncertainty, God's purpose shone through. And what of Jim Elliot and his friends? Did they receive God's promise of meaning and fulfillment in their lives? Did Elisabeth Elliot and her daughter? Yes. Because, in Jim's own words, "He is no fool who gives up what he cannot keep to gain what he cannot lose."[2]

*Heavenly Father, the desires I have to do something significant with my life are not wrong. Those desires are from You! Please help me enflame those urges rather than numb them with comfort or with pleasure. Also, Father, please help me pursue fulfillment and significance through serving You rather than serving myself. In Jesus' name, amen.*

## Next Steps

*Which Bible passage mentioned in this chapter feels most meaningful to you in connection with God's promise of purpose? Write out that passage in the space below.*

---

---

---

---

---

---

---

---

---

---

---

---

---

*What step can you take this week to receive*
*God's promise of purpose?*

_____

_____

_____

_____

_____

_____

_____

_____

_____

_____

_____

_____

_____

_____

_____

_____

_____

_____

CHAPTER SIX

# GOD PROMISES YOU
# RELATIONSHIP

*For the LORD loves justice,*
*And does not forsake His saints;*
*They are preserved forever,*
*But the descendants of the wicked shall be cut off.*
*The righteous shall inherit the land,*
*And dwell in it forever.*
Psalm 37:28–29

EVERYTHING STARTED WHEN LOUIS JORDAN, AGE thirty-seven, lost his job. Needing a change of scenery, he moved onto his thirty-five-foot sailboat at a small marina on the coast of South Carolina. He spent months rehabbing the fifty-year-old vessel, making it seaworthy. During that time he foraged for wild food and lived off the many fish he netted in the Intracoastal Waterway.

On January 23, 2015, Jordan sailed his boat, *Angel*, into the open ocean, where he spent the next sixty-six days alone—although not by choice.

Jordan's parents had kept in touch with their son after his move. They knew he'd gone sailing, but when they didn't hear from him for more than six days, they contacted the Coast Guard. Despite nearly two weeks of searching and broadcasting alert bulletins among maritime commercial companies, no one saw any signs of Louis Jordan or his sailboat. The Coast Guard even checked banking and other financial records up and down the East Coast to see if perhaps he had put in at another harbor and failed to notify his family. Nothing. It was as if Jordan had vanished into thin air—or sunk beneath the surface.

Enter the thousand-foot German shipping vessel *Houston Express* on April 2—a full sixty-six days after Jordan left the South Carolina marina. Sailing two hundred miles off the coast of North Carolina, the crew spotted a man sitting on top of what appeared to be a capsized boat. The German ship stopped, deployed a small rescue craft, and plucked Jordan off his upside-down sailboat. Within three hours, a Coast Guard rescue helicopter retrieved him from the deck of the container ship.

Can you imagine spending sixty-six days alone on the ocean? Louis Jordan caught fish and saved rainwater to sustain himself. He broke a bone in his shoulder when the ship capsized, but he was otherwise unharmed. Spiritually and emotionally, he gave credit to prayer and the Bible for sustaining him through the ordeal: "When you hear about people surviving a long time, in hard conditions, they always [credit] the Bible. That's the main thing that keeps people going. Power—there's power in that like nothing else."[1]

Amen to that! The Bible is "living and powerful . . . and is a discerner of the thoughts and intents of the heart" (Hebrews 4:12). Thankfully, Louis Jordan knew to rely on the promises of God's Word.

I hope you're also learning the power of those promises as we make our way through these pages. No matter what we face, God's Word can bring us through.

Still, I'd like you to think about what was going through Louis Jordan's mind when he realized he was stuck in the middle of the ocean without any way to contact another human being. Can you imagine the sense of isolation and aloneness? Can you imagine the silence as the waves rocked the boat up and down, up and down? Can you imagine the darkness in the deepest parts of all sixty-five nights?

The human fear of living and dying alone has been a constant theme in literature and film, and for good reason: "It is not good that man should be alone" (Genesis 2:18). Human beings are hardwired for company, for relationships, for interaction, and for love. As much as we crave a few moments of peace, or even a couple days of "alone time," we reach our limit pretty quickly. This is all the more true in our digital age, when we are often tethered to devices that keep us from losing touch.

Yet being alone happens—if not by choice, then

No matter what we face, God's Word can bring us through.

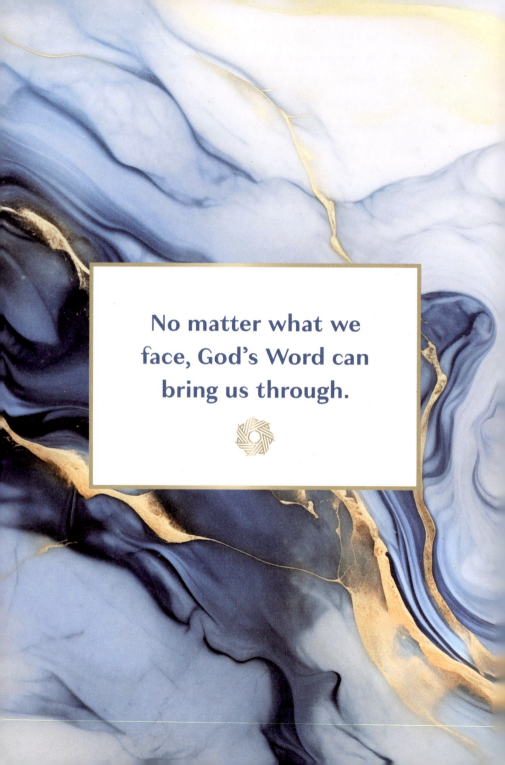

sometimes by circumstance. We may not be adrift on the ocean for two months, but we can feel adrift from relationships, from purpose, from direction, and from our community. When that happens, we can even be tempted to think we've been set adrift from God Himself.

When you struggle with that kind of loneliness or feelings of isolation, I want you to remember this promise: In Christ we are never alone.

We've been exploring Psalm 37 throughout these pages, and David made reference to that promise when he wrote, "The LORD loves justice, and does not forsake His saints" (v. 28).

How did David know that God does not forsake His saints? Because he had experienced that vital connection and life-saving relationship many times. Remember, David found himself isolated as an outcast on several occasions throughout his life, even to the point of being physically hunted by King Saul and his armies. In those moments, David felt deeply and utterly alone. Even so, he always knew he could reach out to God.

In his words:

> The pangs of death surrounded me,
> And the floods of ungodliness made me
>    afraid.
> The sorrows of Sheol surrounded me;
> The snares of death confronted me.

In my distress I called upon the LORD,
And cried out to my God;
He heard my voice from His temple,
And my cry came before Him, even to His
ears. (Psalm 18:4–6)

God has promised to maintain a real, vital relationship with you. He has promised to remain connected to you no matter what else happens in your life—not just every now and then, but all the time. This is a connection you can rely on every single day.

Let's take a closer look at that promise and how you and I can receive it in our lives.

## Recognizing God's Promise of Relationship

I don't know if there's a lonelier moment in Scripture than what the prophet Elijah experienced in the book of 1 Kings. To give some context, God inspired Elijah to confront evil King Ahab with this declaration: "As the LORD God of Israel lives, before whom I stand, there shall not be dew nor rain these years, except at my word" (17:1).

What a promise! Actually, what a threat! If Elijah was wrong and rain watered the ground, he would be mocked as a false prophet. If he was correct, he would be hated by the leaders of an agrarian society that was completely dependent on rain to grow crops. He was in a no-win situation.

Knowing this, God told him, "Get away from here and turn eastward, and hide by the Brook Cherith, which flows into the Jordan. And it will be that you shall drink from the brook, and I have commanded the ravens to feed you there" (vv. 3–4).

Elijah did as God told him. He camped out by the Brook Cherith for months, possibly for years. He was completely isolated, with only ravens to visit him and bring food twice a day. Then, when the brook dried up because of the drought, God sent Elijah to the foreign town of Zarephath, where he stayed with a young widow and her son. He'd left the brook, but he still had to hide in the midst of a hostile people.

After *three long years*, Elijah finally came out of hiding and presented himself to King Ahab. That resulted in the famous confrontation on Mount Carmel, where Elijah triumphed over 850 false prophets and after which God once again opened the heavens so that rain could fall on Israel.

That was an amazing moment for both the people and the prophet, but what do we find in the very next chapter? Elijah was back on his own, isolated once more. The rest of the land was starving for food and water, but Elijah the prophet was starving for relationship. For connection. Look at what he told God: "I have been very zealous for the LORD God of hosts; because the children of Israel have forsaken Your covenant, torn down Your altars, and killed Your prophets with the sword. *I alone am left; and they seek to take my life*" (19:14, emphasis added).

How did God respond? First, He invited Elijah into a deeply personal conversation. He brough Elijah up to a cave and spoke with him in "a still small voice" (v. 12).

Second, God showed Elijah that he wasn't alone:

> "Also you shall anoint Jehu the son of Nimshi as king over Israel. And Elisha the son of Shaphat of Abel Meholah you shall anoint as prophet in your place. It shall be that whoever escapes the sword of Hazael, Jehu will kill; and whoever escapes the sword of Jehu, Elisha will kill. Yet I have reserved seven thousand in Israel, all whose knees have not bowed to Baal, and every mouth that has not kissed him." (vv. 16–18)

Jehu was God's instrument to destroy the house of King Ahab and Jezebel, and also to further eradicate the practice of Baal worship within Israel. Elisha became a disciple of Elijah, with whom he had lived, serving him and learning from him. More than that, to show Elijah that he wasn't alone, God revealed to him that there were still seven thousand devout men of faith who chased after righteousness in Israel.

Here's the point of this story: Even when Elijah *felt* deeply alone, he wasn't alone. God was with him. And God worked through a number of circumstances to bring people into Elijah's life who provided genuine fellowship and meaningful connection.

God has promised a similar relationship for you and me. No matter what we may experience or encounter in our lives, we can know for certain that we are never truly alone:

- "Yea, though I walk through the valley of the shadow of death, I will fear no evil; for You are with me; Your rod and Your staff, they comfort me" (Psalm 23:4).
- "When you pass through the waters, I will be with you; and through the rivers, they shall not overflow you. When you walk through the fire, you shall not be burned, nor shall the flame scorch you. For I am the LORD your God, the Holy One of Israel, your Savior" (Isaiah 43:2–3).
- "Jesus came and spoke to them, saying, 'All authority has been given to Me in heaven and on earth. Go therefore and make disciples of all the nations, baptizing them in the name of the Father and of the Son and of the Holy Spirit, teaching them to observe all things that I have commanded you; *and lo, I am with you always, even to the end*

*of the age.'* Amen" (Matthew 28:18–20, emphasis added).

- "I will pray the Father, and He will give you another Helper, that He may abide with you forever—the Spirit of truth, whom the world cannot receive, because it neither sees Him nor knows Him; but you know Him, for He dwells with you and will be in you. I will not leave you orphans; I will come to you" (John 14:16–18).

## Receiving God's Promise of Relationship

Some may read these pages and ask, "What's the big deal? Some people feel lonely every now and again, but that's not a real problem, is it?"

Actually, loneliness *is* a real problem. In fact, a recent report by the surgeon general of the United States showed that chronic loneliness is as harmful to our bodies as smoking fifteen cigarettes a day! Loneliness is destructive and deadly, and not just for individuals. That same report indicated that our health industry spends billions of dollars every year to combat the physical harm caused by loneliness in this country.

In the words of the surgeon general: "We now know that loneliness is a common feeling that many people experience. It's like hunger or thirst. It's a feeling the body sends us when something we need for survival is missing."[2]

Let's take a moment to clarify our terms. There is a difference between *being alone* (which is a fact) and *feeling alone* (which is a feeling). Those things don't always happen together. We can be alone without feeling alone, and we can feel alone without being alone. (Or, if we're adrift on the Atlantic Ocean like Louis Jordan, we can be and feel alone at the same time.)

Many characters in the Bible found themselves physically alone at different points in their lives. Adam was alone in the garden of Eden; Moses was alone when he fled from Egypt into the wilderness; Joseph was alone in the cistern where his brothers threw him; David was alone when tending his father's flocks as a teenage shepherd and later when he fled from Saul; Daniel was alone in a lion's den, and his three friends were alone in a furnace; Elijah was alone in a cave on Mount Horeb; the prophets were often alone; Jonah was alone under a vine in Nineveh; Jesus was alone in the wilderness and on the cross; Paul was alone in prison. The list goes on.

These biblical characters were *in fact* alone at times in their lives. In that way, they illustrate what is common to all of us: There will be times when we are alone in life. All of us will deal with times of isolation and loneliness.

However, what we can learn from those biblical examples is that feeling alone doesn't have to lead to the

We can view
loneliness as a signal
that it's time to run
toward God and seek
His companionship.

devastating consequences that often accompany loneliness. Instead of allowing the feeling of loneliness to drive us into harmful thoughts or behaviors, we can view that loneliness as a signal that it's time for us to find what we need.

Specifically, we can view loneliness as a signal that it's time to run toward God and seek His companionship.

Again, our examples from Scripture felt alone—probably intensely alone at times. But when their feelings became a signal, they called out to God. They knew they were not *actually* alone in life regardless of how they felt. They knew that God was just a prayer away. In a pit, in a cave, in a lions' den or furnace, in a wilderness, in prison, or on a cross, these mentors of ours did not allow their feelings to conquer their faith.

What about the times when you feel alone in spite of being surrounded by other people and activity? That probably describes more and more of us in a crowded world full of "intimate strangers." Whether we are actually alone or not, feelings of aloneness can create that most threatening of experiences. "Most threatening" because it is the opposite of that for which God created us: attachment and relationship.

It's in those moments, when feelings of aloneness make us question ourselves as well as God, that we need to focus on a different faith-based fact: In Christ we are never alone.

Let's camp on that concept of "fact" for a moment,

because the Christian life is a fact-based, not just feeling-based, relationship with God. Let me point out five important facts that can ground us in our connection with God whenever we may feel alone.

*Fact #1: You aren't meant to be alone.* Aloneness was the only thing in the garden of Eden that God said was "not good." God wants us to enjoy His company and the company of others (Genesis 2:18). Therefore, it's right for you to invest effort into relationships not only with God but also with people. That's what you were designed to enjoy.

*Fact #2: God is everywhere.* David wrote a psalm about the impossibility of escaping God's presence, in which he penned these words:

> Where can I go from Your Spirit?
> Or where can I flee from Your presence?
> If I ascend into heaven, You are there;
> If I make my bed in hell, behold, You are there.
> If I take the wings of the morning,
> And dwell in the uttermost parts of the sea,
> Even there Your hand shall lead me,
> And Your right hand shall hold me. (Psalm
> 139:7–10)

Whether you are a Christian or not, you are never alone because God is wherever you are.

*Fact #3: Jesus is always with His disciples.* I mentioned the Great Commission earlier in the chapter, but I want to repeat it here because of Jesus' promise at the end:

> "Go therefore and make disciples of all the nations, baptizing them in the name of the Father and of the Son and of the Holy Spirit, teaching them to observe all things that I have commanded you; and lo, I am with you always, even to the end of the age." (Matthew 28:19–20)

God is everywhere. However, Jesus promised to be "with" His disciples in a way that transcends even God's omnipresence. If you are a follower of Jesus Christ, then He is with you at all times—with you to support you, comfort you, teach you, and lift you up. How long will that reality last? Even to the end of the age.

*Fact #4: God will never forsake you.* God promised His people in the Old and New Testaments that He would never leave or forsake them. This is a promise He gave over and over, including in Deuteronomy 31:6, Joshua 1:5, and Hebrews 13:5.

God will never leave you, abandon you, or turn His back on you. You can take that promise to the bank.

*Fact #5: You can fight back against loneliness.* I'm afraid people often view loneliness in the same way they view their height or the number of toes on their feet. That

If you are a follower of Jesus Christ, then He is with you at all times—with you to support you, comfort you, teach you, and lift you up. How long will that reality last? Even to the end of the age.

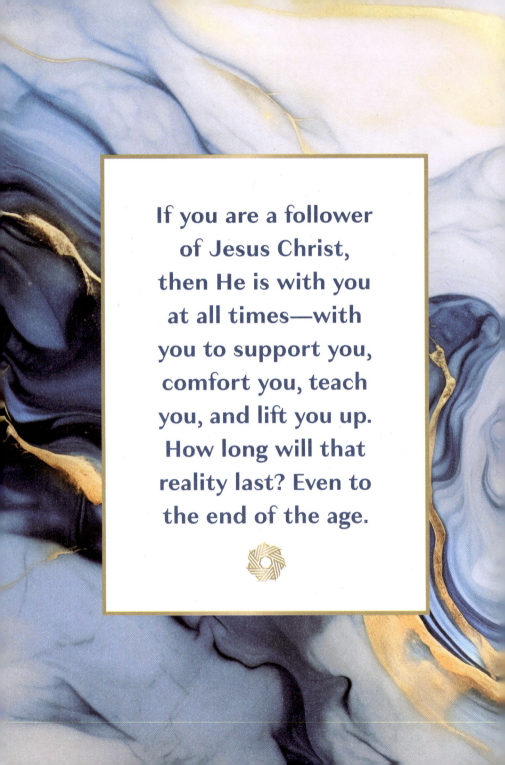

is, we often perceive loneliness as something outside our control.

That's not correct. We can press back against the loneliness epidemic in our nation, in our communities, and in our lives. How do we fight against loneliness? It starts with faith, which is choosing to believe the truths we've outlined in this chapter. That is how we dispel feelings of loneliness when they surface in our lives.

Most people associate being a professional athlete with a lot of glory and glamour, and there's certainly some truth to that perception. But reality can be different for many hockey players who participate in a grueling schedule that packs eighty-two physically demanding games into a seven-month regular season.

Life on the road can be tough. It's time away from family and friends. Time away from a church community. Time away from friends.

Casey DeSmith has experienced that grind for several seasons as the star goalie for the Dallas Stars, but he has discovered a secret in recent years that helps him make it through. "For me, recently . . . the biggest development in my faith was realizing how much God just wants to be my friend and have a relationship with me," he said. "That is, in the end, most important to Him, and that should be most important to me as well."

For DeSmith, the eternal nature of our relationship with God is especially astounding: "It's eternity. It's forever. It's the most important decision that you'll ever make. It's the most important friendship you'll ever have. I have some amazing friends, but none of them in reality are as important as God—as my relationship and my friendship with God."[3]

You and I are more likely to *feel* alone than we are to *be* alone. Even if both happen at the same time, we must remember: In Christ we are never alone.

*Heavenly Father, You will never leave me nor forsake me. I choose to hold on to that promise no matter what else happens in my life. Please remind me of that promise when I feel lonely, and please reach out to me through Your Spirit whenever I feel like I'm on my own. In Jesus' name, amen.*

## Next Steps

*Which Bible passage mentioned in this chapter feels most meaningful to you in connection with God's promise of relationship and connection? Write out that passage in the space below.*

_____

_____

_____

_____

_____

_____

_____

_____

_____

_____

_____

_____

*What step can you take this week to receive*
*God's promise of a relationship with Him?*

_____

_____

_____

_____

_____

_____

_____

_____

_____

_____

_____

_____

_____

_____

_____

_____

# CHAPTER SEVEN

# GOD PROMISES YOU
# ETERNITY

*But the salvation of the righteous is from the L*ORD*;*
*He is their strength in the time of trouble.*

Psalm 37:39

ONLY A HANDFUL OF SONGS ARE SO ICONIC THAT everyone knows them.

"Over the Rainbow" is one of those songs. It spun around the world like a tornado when Judy Garland, playing the role of Dorothy, sang it in the 1939 movie *The Wizard of* Oz. In an early scene, Dorothy and her dog, Toto, have a run-in with an unpleasant woman. When Dorothy tells her family about it, her Aunt Em suggests that she go and find herself a place where she won't get into any trouble.

As she and Toto walk away, Dorothy says, "Do you suppose there is such a place, Toto? There must be. It's not a place you can get to by a boat, or a train. It's far, far away. Behind the moon, beyond the rain." Then she breaks into song: "Somewhere over the rainbow, way up high."[1]

Decades later, the song was introduced to a new generation by the "Voice of Hawaii"—singer and ukulele player Israel "IZ" Kamakawiwo'ole, a Christian, who passed away in 1997.

It's interesting that the same hit, performed very differently by two musical superstars, could stir the hearts of two generations. The reason goes beyond the song's evocative melody, for its words transcend the human heart and express a deep yearning for a better place than we currently have.

There's another poignant layer to the story of the song. The lyrics were penned by Yip Harburg, and the musical score was written by Harold Arlen. Both were Jewish. Harburg was the son of Russian-Jewish immigrants who grew up in a Yiddish-speaking Orthodox Jewish home in New York. Arlen's family had emigrated from Lithuania.

Now remember, this was 1939—a time when Jews in Europe were facing unspeakable danger. Anti-Semitism covered Europe like an ugly shroud. Jewish people were persecuted, isolated, threatened, and rounded up like animals.

Harburg and Arlen were born in the safety of America,

but their hearts were at home. They wanted to write a song of hope, for they longed for the day when things would be better—that skies would be blue and the dark clouds would disappear. When they wrote about flying high over the chimney tops or being found beyond the rainbow, they couldn't have known how heartrending their words would be during the terrors of the Nazi death camps, where six million Jews were executed and destroyed in mass crematoriums.[2]

It's in the human bloodstream to long for a better place—to ache for a place way up high where the dreams you dare to dream really do come true. We won't find fulfillment for that longing in America or Israel or any other geographical location, not on this side of the rapture. But God has promised to bring all His children into a glorious future on His terms and in His timing.

Ultimately, heaven is where our hopes will be fulfilled.

David pointed to that future at the end of Psalm 37:

> Mark the blameless man, and observe the
>     upright;
> For the future of that man is peace. . . .
> The salvation of the righteous is from
>     the LORD;
> He is their strength in the time of trouble.
>     (vv. 37, 39)

It's in the human bloodstream to long for a better place.

God has promised all believers a future filled with "peace." This future is accessed not through money or status or celebrity or ethnicity; we can enter heaven only through "the salvation of the righteous," which comes from "the LORD."

Do you feel confident in God's promise of salvation? You can! We're going to learn more about that promise in this chapter—and I think it's likely you may be surprised by what you read! We'll also identify a few active, practical steps you and I can take to live in the reality of eternity not just tomorrow but also today. In fact, right now.

## Recognizing God's Promise of Eternity

The only reliable source of information about eternity is the Bible—the Word of God. Our heavenly Father couldn't wait for us to join Him in heaven, so He filled His Book with information we can read, study, and use as a basis for anticipation. Every word of God's Book is true, sure, and guaranteed by the resurrection of Jesus, who has gone ahead to prepare a place for us.

That certainly includes all the promises Scripture contains about heaven. Here are some of the most famous examples:

- "For God so loved the world that He gave His only begotten Son, that whoever believes in Him should not perish but have everlasting life. For God did not send His Son into the world to condemn the world, but that the world through Him might be saved" (John 3:16–17).
- "In My Father's house are many mansions; if it were not so, I would have told you. I go to prepare a place for you. And if I go and prepare a place for you, I will come again and receive you to Myself; that where I am, there you may be also" (John 14:2–3).
- "For we know that if our earthly house, this tent, is destroyed, we have a building from God, a house not made with hands, eternal in the heavens. For in this we groan, earnestly desiring to be clothed with our habitation which is from heaven" (2 Corinthians 5:1–2).
- "Therefore, since all these things will be dissolved, what manner of persons ought you to be in holy conduct and godliness, looking for and hastening the coming of the day of God, because of which the heavens will be dissolved, being on fire, and the elements will melt with fervent heat? Nevertheless we, according to His promise, look for new heavens and a new earth in which righteousness dwells" (2 Peter 3:11–13).

Here's an important question: When will you and I experience heaven? Most people believe the answer is "As soon as I die." Right? That's the impression we often get from church or from evangelism training. We tell others they need to be saved so that they can go to heaven when they die.

But here's something that might surprise you: Believers in Jesus don't go to heaven immediately after they die. At least we don't go to the version of heaven we think of as "eternity." Not yet.

Let me walk through the timeline of our heavenly future according to God's Word. First, if you or I were to pass away right now, our physical bodies would remain behind here on earth while our soul would be transported to paradise. You've heard that term in the pages of Scripture, most notably when Jesus spoke to the believing criminal who was crucified next to Him: "Assuredly, I say to you, today you will be with Me in Paradise" (Luke 23:43).

Paradise is similar to heaven in that it is a spiritual place in which God dwells with Jesus, with His angels, and with other spiritual beings. Paul described being "caught up into Paradise" and hearing "inexpressible words, which it is not lawful for a man to utter" (2 Corinthians 12:4). John spoke of it in the book of Revelation when he described this message from Jesus to the church at Ephesus: "He who has an ear, let him hear what the Spirit says to the churches. To him who overcomes I will give to eat from the tree of life, which is in the midst of the Paradise of God" (2:7).

So paradise is similar to what we think of as heaven, but it is not eternal in the way heaven will be. More on that in a moment.

Now, let's say you and I were to be on this earth when the rapture takes place. And oh, I do hope that will be the case! If so, we will be caught up with Jesus and taken to paradise to join all the believers who already passed away. Paul wrote about that moment to encourage the early church:

> For the Lord Himself will descend from heaven with a shout, with the voice of an archangel, and with the trumpet of God. And the dead in Christ will rise first. Then we who are alive and remain shall be caught up together with them in the clouds to meet the Lord in the air. And thus we shall always be with the Lord. (1 Thessalonians 4:16–17)

Everyone who is a believer in Jesus will remain in paradise throughout the entirety of the tribulation. That's the period of seven years during which God will bring judgment on the earth against Satan, his demons, and every human being who has rebelled against Him.

Thankfully, we will have no part in those seven years of terror. We will be with Christ.

Then, at the end of the tribulation, Jesus will return to earth in an event we often refer to as the second coming. That will be an awesome moment in every sense of the word. Jesus will conquer the Antichrist and the armies of the earth, and He will take His rightful place as King.

Will that be the moment we go to heaven in the eternal sense? Surprisingly, no. That's because the second coming of Jesus will usher in a completely new phase of human history on this planet. That phase is called the millennium, which will be a true golden age for humankind.

What is the millennium? The apostle John described it well in the book of Revelation:

> Then I saw an angel coming down from heaven, having the key to the bottomless pit and a great chain in his hand. He laid hold of the dragon, that serpent of old, who is the Devil and Satan, and bound him for a thousand years; and he cast him into the bottomless pit, and shut him up, and set a seal on him, so that he should deceive the nations no more till the thousand years were finished. But after these things he must be released for a little while.

> Everyone who is a believer in Jesus will remain in paradise throughout the entirety of the tribulation. That's the period of seven years during which God will bring judgment on the earth against Satan, his demons, and every human being who has rebelled against Him.

And I saw thrones, and they sat on them, and judgment was committed to them. Then I saw the souls of those who had been beheaded for their witness to Jesus and for the word of God, who had not worshiped the beast or his image, and had not received his mark on their foreheads or on their hands. And they lived and reigned with Christ for a thousand years. But the rest of the dead did not live again until the thousand years were finished. This is the first resurrection. Blessed and holy is he who has part in the first resurrection. Over such the second death has no power, but they shall be priests of God and of Christ, and shall reign with Him a thousand years. (20:1–6)

Importantly, the millennium will be a physical expression of God's kingdom here on earth. It will not be a time when people sit on clouds and play harps up in the sky. Instead, we will live, work, play, rest, and worship as human beings in perfected human bodies. We will do so under the kingship of Jesus, who will reign from His throne in Jerusalem. And we will experience that reign for a thousand years, during which Satan and his demons will be completely absent.

For all those reasons and more, the millennium will be another version of paradise. It will be a time of joy and prosperity, safety and worship unlike anything we've seen so far.

But that time will come to an end:

Now when the thousand years have expired, Satan will be released from his prison and will go out to deceive the nations which are in the four corners of the earth, Gog and Magog, to gather them together to battle, whose number is as the sand of the sea. They went up on the breadth of the earth and surrounded the camp of the saints and the beloved city. And fire came down from God out of heaven and devoured them. (vv. 7–9)

The millennium will end in a second fall—a second rebellion against God. Afterward, the heavens and the earth will be reforged. Only then will we experience the truly eternal nature of God's kingdom we typically think of when we think about "heaven."

John described that eternity for us near the end of Revelation:

And he showed me a pure river of water of life, clear as crystal, proceeding from the throne of God and of the Lamb. In the middle of its street, and on either side of the river, was the tree of life, which bore twelve fruits, each tree yielding its fruit every month. The leaves of the tree were for the healing of the nations. And there shall be no more curse, but the throne of God and of the Lamb shall be in it, and His servants shall serve Him. They shall see His face, and His name shall be on their foreheads. There shall be no night there: They need no lamp nor light of the sun, for the Lord God gives them light. And they shall reign forever and ever. (22:1–5)

That's what heaven will be like. And that's what God has promised to all who choose to follow Him— including you.

## Receiving God's Promise of Eternity

How do we receive the promise of eternity in our hearts and minds? By anticipating the reality of heaven. By fixing our thoughts and our desires on the glory of what is to come.

Writing to the Christians in Philippi, Paul lamented those who called themselves believers yet refused to live their lives from a heavenly perspective. Such people were "enemies of the cross of Christ" because their end was their destruction, their god was their bellies, and their glory was their shame. In short, they "set their mind on earthly things" (Philippians 3:18–19).

In contrast, Paul encouraged the believers of the early church—and by extension, all believers—to set our minds on things above:

For our citizenship is in heaven, from which we also eagerly wait for the Savior, the Lord Jesus Christ,

How do we receive
the promise of
eternity in our
hearts and minds?
By anticipating the
reality of heaven. By
fixing our thoughts
and our desires
on the glory of
what is to come.

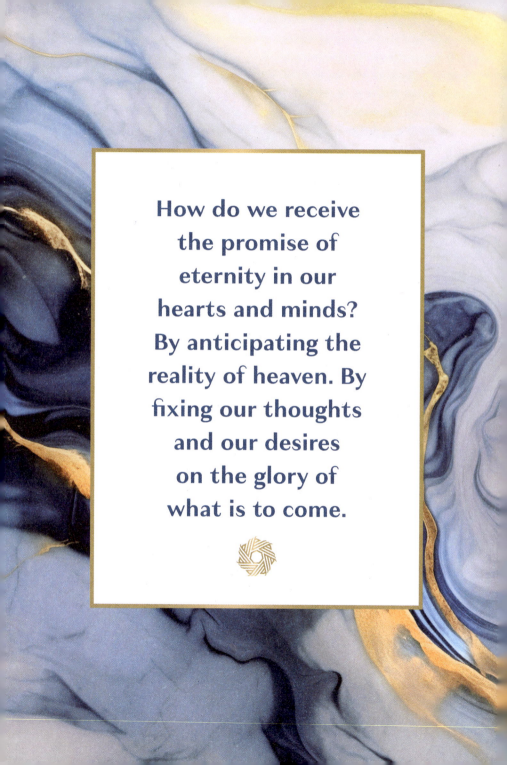

who will transform our lowly body that it may be conformed to His glorious body, according to the working by which He is able even to subdue all things to Himself. (vv. 20–21)

You and I can receive the promise of eternity right now when we meditate on the reality of heaven, when we marinate ourselves in the glory of heaven, and when we mature ourselves by refusing to be dragged into the muck and the mire of earthly concerns. Does that mean we neglect our mortgage or refuse to take out the garbage? No. It means we make eternity our primary concern.

Here are several specific truths about heaven you can use to fill your mind and your heart as you "eagerly wait for the Savior, the Lord Jesus Christ."

*Anticipate the peace of heaven.* We talked about the peace God promises His children in chapter 3, but it's important for us to remember that heaven will be a place where we don't have to strive for peace. We will simply receive it and enjoy it as a gift from our good Father. Just as important, that peace will pervade the entirety of heaven. Every place we go will be a bastion of serenity and calm.

As Peter told us, "Therefore, beloved, looking forward to these things, be diligent to be found by Him in peace" (2 Peter 3:14).

*Anticipate the health of heaven.* Oliviah Hall was only

a child when she was diagnosed with a rare form of brain cancer. For sixteen months, she encouraged multitudes of people and changed lives. She sang hymns and shared her faith. Thanks to the A Special Wish Foundation, she got to be an honorary reporter for a local television station, toured the FBI headquarters in Washington, got to know members of the Secret Service, and even met President Donald Trump. When she passed away at age ten, she was given a farewell salute by more than twenty law enforcement officials. Her pastor said she had changed people's lives forever.

One Easter, sometime before her illness, Oliviah had asked Christ into her life, and she flourished in her fellowship with Him. Her stated attitude about her illness was this: She told others if she wasn't healed in this world, she would be healed in heaven.[3]

What Oliviah believed is what the Bible teaches. Namely, heaven will be a place of perfect health and strength. A place where we will no longer face disease or crying or pain.

Isn't that a promise you can hold in your mind today?

***Anticipate the safety of heaven.*** Heaven will also be a place of safety. It's disturbing to realize there is no truly safe square inch on our planet—except in the pathway of God's will for each of us, and even then we're not promised absolute physical safety. Our planet is unstable, unsafe, and prone to unexpected dangers.

> Heaven will be a
> place of perfect
> health and strength.
> A place where we
> will no longer face
> disease or crying
> or pain. Isn't that
> a promise you
> can hold in your
> mind today?

But listen to this: "He who dwells in the secret place of the Most High shall abide under the shadow of the Almighty" (Psalm 91:1).

*Anticipate the joy of heaven.* The Bible also promises that heaven will be a place of joy. Psalm 16:11 says, "You will show me the path of life; in Your presence is fullness of joy; at Your right hand are pleasures forevermore."

When we ask Christ to come into our heart, the Holy Spirit brings joy and the assurance of our salvation into our heart, which gives us a glimpse of what is to come in heaven one day (Ephesians 1:13–14). Think about that! Whenever you experience an attitude of joy now, it's a preview of the limitless joy you'll experience in heaven. Your present joy is brought to you in advance by the Holy Spirit, but your future joy will have no end.

*Anticipate the reunions of heaven.* One of the greatest joys of heaven will be our reunion with those who preceded us to the Celestial City. A lot of us are homesick for eternity because we have so many loved ones who have gone before us.

Well, here's the truth: We will see them again! We will know them again. In fact, we will know them and love them and be loved by them in ways far more perfect than we ever experienced here on earth.

*The Christian Post* once asked evangelist Billy Graham if we'll have trouble being reunited with our loved ones in heaven because millions and millions of people will be there. This was his reply:

Yes, there will be a vast number of people in heaven, for every person through the ages who has trusted Christ for their salvation will be there. The Bible says that because of Christ's death for us, heaven will be filled with "a great multitude that

A lot of us are homesick for eternity because we have so many loved ones who have gone before us. Well, here's the truth: We will see them again!

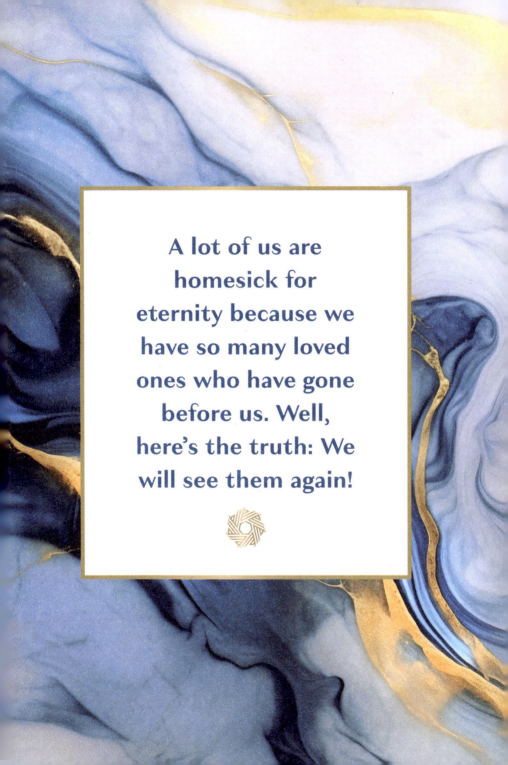

no one could count, from every nation, tribe, people and language. . . ." But you shouldn't worry about getting lost, or never finding your loved ones in heaven—not at all. If God brought you together on this earth—out of all the billions of people who live here now—will He be able to bring you together in heaven? Of course.[4]

The world today is filled with threats. We have so many reasons to worry and feel unsafe. But don't let your mind become dragged down by earthly things. Set your thoughts on the promise of eternity and all that God has in store.

*Heavenly Father, I confess that it's easy for me to dwell on earthly things each day. I am often pushed and pulled by pressures and desires that have no impact on eternity. I confess my wrong focus, Father, and I choose right now to make You the center of my thoughts for the rest of this day. You are my most important priority for now and for all eternity. In Jesus' name, amen.*

## Next Steps

*Which Bible passage mentioned in this chapter feels most meaningful to you in connection with God's promise of eternal life? Write out that passage in the space below.*

_____

_____

_____

_____

_____

_____

_____

_____

_____

_____

_____

_____

*What step can you take this week to receive*
*God's promise of eternity?*

_____

_____

_____

_____

_____

_____

_____

_____

_____

_____

_____

_____

_____

_____

_____

_____

_____

# YOUR PROMISE TO GOD

**IT WAS THE AFTERNOON OF SEPTEMBER 12, 1962.**
Tens of thousands of people had packed themselves into
the football stadium of Rice University near Houston,
Texas. The atmosphere was expectant and excited as
people stood or chatted together in the heat. Women
and men regularly glanced toward the stage set up
on the field, even as children played or ran around
behind them.

Then, after a huge round of applause, President John
F. Kennedy stood behind the podium and began to speak.

The specific subject of that speech was the "space

race" between the United States and the Soviet Union—a major topic in that day and time. The US was lagging behind in that race and needed a boost in order to regain the lead. Without being overly technical, the president acknowledged reality and explained some of the steps he and other national leaders planned to take as a way of rectifying the situation.

But JFK's speech that day was about more than policy. It was about a promise. Namely, the president made a bold commitment that both inspired the American people and changed the fate of our nation. Here it is:

> We choose to go to the Moon. We choose to go to the Moon in this decade and do the other things, not because they are easy, but because they are hard, because that goal will serve to organize and measure the best of our energies and skills, because that challenge is one that we are willing to accept, one we are unwilling to postpone, and one which we intend to win.[1]

The president's promise was clear: America would send a man to the moon. That promise was also specific and timely, as he clarified later in the speech: "This will be done in the decade of the sixties. It may be done while some of you are still here at school at this college and university. It will be done during the term of office of some of the people who sit here on this platform. But it will be done. And it will be done before the end of this decade."[2]

An assassin's bullet robbed President Kennedy of the chance to see that promise fulfilled. But his early efforts and his inspiring vision are what made that fulfillment possible. On July 16, 1969, the United States did send two astronauts to the moon—an achievement many believed to be impossible on the day of Kennedy's speech.

As we've seen throughout these pages, our heavenly Father has made many promises to His children, and He has kept them all. He *will* keep them all. We can take them to the bank.

How, then, should we respond to those promises? How should we respond to God's faithfulness to us? Gratitude is certainly a good starting place. But I'd like to conclude these pages by offering four specific steps you and I can take each day in light of God's fulfilled promises. These are three commitments we can strive to keep for Him *because of* the way God keeps His commitments to us.

First, we must commit ourselves to following God's will and God's plan for our lives—and those last three words are significant. For *our* lives. Yours for you and mine for me. Don't look at others and compare yourself, saying, "His opportunity is better or bigger." Or "I could do a lot better if I was in her shoes." God has created a one-of-a-kind design for your life, and He assigns your tasks daily.

When the Christians in the city of Corinth started to argue about which of their leaders was best, Paul responded with a severe rebuke: "What, after all, is Apollos? And what is Paul? Only servants, through whom you came to believe—as the Lord has assigned to each his task. I planted the seed, Apollos watered it, but God has been making it grow. So neither the one who plants nor the one who waters is anything, but only God, who makes things grow" (1 Corinthians 3:5–7 NIV).

Notice the words "as the Lord has assigned to each his task." God has given you many gifts and placed you in the circumstances He has chosen. Your job is to follow His will and plan for your life. Committing to that plan is a logical response to His faithfulness in your life.

Second, we must commit to the right attitude, which is the heart of a servant. Notice how Paul put it in the passage above: We are "only servants." Not *just* servants, but *only* servants. That's all we are. When we wake up in the morning, shower, dress, and walk out the door, our mindset should be: How can I serve God today, and how can I serve those who I meet?

Imagine going into each day trying to find a quiet way of serving everyone who crossed your path. What a response to God's faithfulness that would be!

Third, as God's children, we must be committed to the Lord's overall mission. Listen to Paul's words again: "I planted the seed, Apollos watered it, but God has been making it grow." The Lord has planted His kingdom in this world, and He allows us to help tend it and make it grow. He longs for men, women, and children to become citizens of His kingdom through the preaching and sharing of the gospel.

As we go about our personal ministries, some people see little results—they are planters. Some see gradual progress—they are waterers. Some see a harvest—they are reapers. But God is above it all, creating the growth as each of us does our assigned part.

Has God kept His promises to you? Has He provided for your needs? Has He forgiven your sins? Has He blessed you with peace and security and purpose? Has He remained close and connected to you in spite of your sin? Has He secured a place in heaven for you?

I know the answer to each of those questions is yes. God is faithful. He will do what He promised. Hallelujah!

In return, let's do our best to commit ourselves to God through our everyday lives. Let's follow His plan each day, adopt the heart of a servant, and give all that we have toward advancing His kingdom. Let's make these commitments not because they are easy—but because they are worthwhile.

Let that be your promise to God, and let it start today.

# NOTES

## Introduction

1. "7 Promises of a Promise Keeper," Promise Keepers, accessed January 31, 2025, https://promisekeepers.org/about-us/.

## Chapter 1: God Promises You Provision

1. Jeanne Armstrong, "12 Neighbours Closer to Goal of Building 99 Tiny Homes—but Not Without Growing Pains," CBC, September 25, 2023, https://www.cbc.ca/news /canada/new-brunswick/12-neighbours-tiny-homes-goal -1.6975817.

2. Andy Corbley, "Millionaire Builds 99 Tiny Homes to Cut Homelessness in His Community—He Even Provides Jobs on Site for Them," Good News Network, October 30, 2023,

https://www.goodnewsnetwork.org/millionaire-builds-99-tiny
-homes-to-cut-homelessness-in-his-community-he-even-provides
-jobs-on-site-for-them/.

3. "Financial Happiness," The Currency, November 8, 2023,
   https://www.empower.com/the-currency/money/research
   -financial-happiness.

4. E. Schuyler English, *H. A. Ironside: Ordained of the Lord*
   (Zondervan, 1946), 25.

## Chapter 2: God Promises You Forgiveness

1. Quoted in Jane Leavy, *The Last Boy: Mickey Mantle and the
   End of America's Childhood* (HarperCollins, 2010), 363–64.

2. Rick Weinberg, "58: Mantle, Nearing Death, Laments a
   'Wasted' Life," ESPN, July 12, 2004, http://sports.espn.go.com
   /espn/espn25/story?page=moments/58.

3. Leavy, *The Last Boy*, 380.

4. Gerald R. Ford, "Statement from the Oval Office Sunday,
   September 8, 1974, 10:45 a.m.," Ford Library Museum,
   https://www.fordlibrarymuseum.gov/sites/default/files
   /pdf_documents/library/document/0122/1252066.pdf.

5. Ryann Blackshere, "Widower Forges Friendship with Man in
   Crash That Killed Wife, Unborn Baby," Today, February 3, 2014,
   https://www.today.com/news/man-crash-killed-woman-forges
   -friendship-her-widower-2D12044681.

## Chapter 3: God Promises You Peace

1. Ashley J. DiMella, "'Unluckiest Woman' Evacuates from
   California Wildfires After Surviving Multiple Natural
   Disasters," FoxNews, September 11, 2024, https://www
   .foxnews.com/lifestyle/unluckiest-woman-evacuates
   -california-wildfires-surviving-multiple-natural-disasters.

2. StudyFinds Staff, "Average Person Spends Their Sundays Terrified of the Week Ahead," StudyFinds, September 30, 2024, https://studyfinds.org/spend-sundays-terrified/.

3. Ed Dobson, *Prayers and Promises When Facing a Life-Threatening Illness* (Zondervan, 2007), 29–30.

4. "Residents Flee Angolan Village Invaded by Elephants," Reuters, March 9, 2010, https://www.reuters.com/article/lifestyle/residents -flee-angolan-village-invaded-by-elephants-idUSTRE6283KE/.

## Chapter 4: God Promises You Protection

1. Caitlin McCormack, "Virginia Man Allegedly Attempted to Brazenly Shoplift from Walmart During Holiday 'Shop with a Cop' Event," *New York Post*, December 3, 2024, https://nypost .com/2024/12/03/us-news/virginia-man-allegedly-attempted -to-shoplift-from-walmart-during-shop-with-a-cop-event/.

2. Jim Probasco, "Who Was Charles Ponzi? What Did He Create?," Investopedia, November 16, 2024, https://www.investopedia .com/who-is-charles-ponzi-5216783.

## Chapter 5: God Promises You Purpose

1. Geeta Pandey, "Why an Indian Couple Is Suing Their Son over Grandchildren," BBC, May 13, 2022, https://www.bbc.com /news/world-asia-india-61436179.

2. "About Jim Elliot," Elisabeth Elliot, accessed February 25, 2025, https://elisabethelliot.org/about/jim-elliot/.

## Chapter 6: God Promises You Relationship

1. Steve Almasy, Ed Payne, and Nick Valencia, "Man Rescued After 66 Days at Sea Is 'Utterly Thankful and Grateful,'" CNN, April 3, 2015, http://www.cnn.com/2015/04/02/us/rescued -after-66-days-at-sea/.

2. Amanda Seitz, "Loneliness Poses Health Risks as Deadly as Smoking, U.S. Surgeon General Says," PBS News, May 2, 2023, https://www.pbs.org/newshour/health/loneliness-poses-health-risks-as-deadly-as-smoking-u-s-surgeon-general-says.

3. "Star Goalie Says Knowing Jesus Is the 'Most Important Friendship,'" MovieGuide, November 1, 2024, https://www.movieguide.org/news-articles/stars-goalie-says-knowing-jesus-is-the-most-important-friendship.html.

## Chapter 7: God Promises You Eternity

1. Judy Garland, "Somewhere Over the Rainbow," from *The Wizard of Oz*. Robbins Music Corporation on behalf of MGM, 1939.

2. "The Powerful Message Behind 'Over the Rainbow,'" Christians United for Israel, November 20, 2015, https://www.cufi.org.uk/spotlight/the-powerful-message-behind-over-the-rainbow/.

3. "Cleveland Browns Help Little Girl Arrest Cat Woman," UPI, March 29, 2018, https://www.upi.com/Sports_News/NFL/2018/03/29/Cleveland-Browns-help-little-girl-arrest-Cat-Woman/7071522340725/.

4. Billy Graham, "Reunion with Loved Ones in Heaven?" *The Christian Post*, December 29, 2008, https://www.christianpost.com/news/reunion-with-loved-ones-in-heaven.html.

## Conclusion: Your Promise to God

1. John F. Kennedy, "Address at Rice University on the Nation's Space Effort," John F. Kennedy Presidential

Library and Museum, accessed March 26, 2025, https://www.jfklibrary.org/learn/about-jfk/historic-speeches /address-at-rice-university-on-the-nations-space-effort.

2. John F. Kennedy, "Address at Rice University on the Nation's Space Effort."

# ABOUT THE AUTHOR

**DR. DAVID JEREMIAH IS THE FOUNDER OF TURNING** Point, an international ministry committed to providing Christians with sound Bible teaching through radio and television, the internet, live events, and resource materials and books. He is the author of more than fifty books, including *The Book of Signs, The Great Disappearance, Where Do We Go from Here?,* and *The Coming Golden Age.*

Dr. Jeremiah serves as the senior pastor of Shadow Mountain Community Church in El Cajon, California. He and his wife, Donna, have four children, twelve grandchildren, and one great-grandchild.